Numbers
for iPad & iPad Pro

SEAN KELLS

Questing Vole Press

Numbers for iPad & iPad Pro
by Sean Kells

Editor: Walt Rodale
Proofreader: Diane Yee
Compositor: Kim Frees
Cover: Questing Vole Press

Contents

CHAPTER 1

Getting Started with Numbers

Numbers for the iPhone and iPod touch

This book covers mainly Numbers for the iPad, iPad Pro, and iPad mini. The small-screened version of Numbers for the iPhone and iPod touch has a cramped and slightly rearranged set of controls but otherwise works about the same as the iPad version. Tasks and instructions apply equally—or nearly so—no matter which iDevice you're using. In most cases, you can mentally replace "iPad" with "iPhone" or "iPod touch".

Numbers is the spreadsheet application in Apple's **iWork** suite for iOS. (The other iWork apps are Pages for word processing and Keynote for presentations.) Numbers for iOS lacks the horsepower and features of Numbers for Mac and Microsoft Excel, and it isn't meant to replace them. But it's tuned to work with iOS's multitouch interface and delivers what you expect from spreadsheet software, plus a few Apple-specific touches.

iPad Basics

This section reviews the iPad's Home screen and multitouch gestures. If you need a refresher on other basics, such as syncing with iTunes or connecting to the internet, then refer to the *iPad User Guide* at *help.apple.com/ipad*.

Tip: The text under app icons can be hard to read, particularly with lighter-colored wallpapers; to make the text bold, tap Settings > General > Accessibility > Bold Text. To turn off the 3D parallax effect that makes icons and alerts "float" above the wallpaper when you twist your iPad in space, tap Settings > General > Accessibility > Reduce Motion > On.

The Home screen

After you unlock your iPad, the **Home screen** appears and displays icons for your **applications**, or **apps** (Figure 1.1). The iPad comes with built-in apps (Safari, Mail, and Settings, for example) and you can download more—including Numbers—from the App Store, Apple's online store for iOS applications. If you install lots of apps, new Home screens sprout automatically to display their icons. Put your most frequently used apps in the **dock**, which is visible at the bottom of every Home screen. The row of small **indicator dots** above the dock indicates how many screens you have and which one you're on. (You can create up to 11 Home screens.) You can customize the layout of app icons on the Home screen and in the dock.

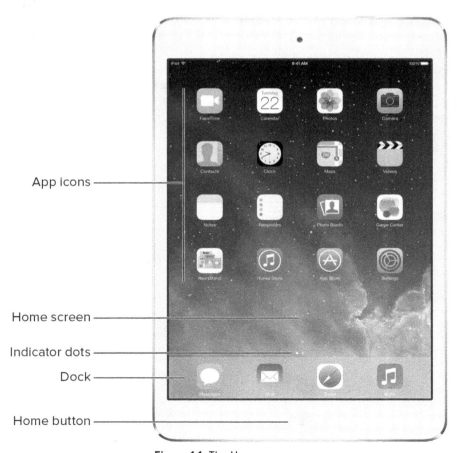

App icons

Home screen

Indicator dots

Dock

Home button

Figure 1.1 The Home screen.

Multitasking

On an iPad, you can use four or five fingers to:

- Pinch to the Home screen

- Flick up to show the multitasking screen

- Flick left or right to switch apps

You can also multitask by using the following features on a newer iPad running iOS 9 or later:

- **Slide Over** overlays a narrow view on the right side of the screen that lets you open a second app without leaving the one you're in. To invoke Slide Over, flick or drag leftward from the right edge of the screen. To open a different secondary app, flick or drag downward from the top edge of the screen on the right side (above the current secondary app), and then tap an app in the list that appears. To dismiss the Slide Over view and get back to the app that you were using before, tap or flick to the left of the Slide Over view.

- **Split View** displays two side-by-side apps, letting you view, resize, and interact with both of them. To invoke Split View, enter Slide Over and then tap or drag the vertical divider control near center screen. Drag the divider left or right to resize the apps, or drag it all the way to the left or right to dismiss one of the apps.

- **Picture in Picture** (sometimes called PiP) lets you play video in a moveable, resizable, mini-window that floats over other open apps. To invoke Picture in Picture, press the Home button while you're playing video (in FaceTime or the Videos app, for example). The video window scales down to a corner of your screen. Tap to open a second app, and your video continues to play while you use the other app.

Tip: To toggle multitasking features, tap Settings > General > Multitasking.

To show the Home screen:

- Do any of the following:

  ► Press the Home button.

  ► Use four or five fingers to pinch to the Home screen.

To switch Home screens:

- Do any of the following:

  ► Flick left or right.

  ► Tap to the left or right of the indicator dots above the dock.

  ► To go to the first Home screen, press the Home button.

To rearrange Home-screen icons:

1 Touch and hold any app icon for a few seconds until all the icons wiggle.

2 Drag icons to new locations within a screen or off the edge of one screen and onto the next.

3 Press the Home button to stop the wiggling and save your arrangement.

To reset the Home screen to its original layout:

- Tap Settings > General > Reset > Reset Home Screen Layout.

Using Multitouch Gestures

As with all iOS apps, you interact with Numbers by using your fingertips to perform the **multitouch gestures**, or simply **gestures**, described in Table 1.1.

The iPad's **capacitive** screen contains a dense grid of touch sensors that responds to the electrical field of your fingers or a capacitive stylus. The screen won't respond to a traditional stylus (and you can't wear ordinary gloves). Increasing finger pressure on a capacitive screen, as opposed to a resistive screen, won't increase responsiveness.

Tips for Multitouch Gestures

- The frame surrounding the screen is called the **bezel**. The bezel doesn't respond to gestures; it's just a place to rest your thumbs.

- Feel free to use two hands. In Numbers, for example, you can use both hands to type on any of the onscreen keyboards. Or you can touch and hold a shape with the finger of one hand, and then use your other hand to tap other shapes to select them all as a group.

- If you're having trouble with a gesture, make sure that you're not touching the screen's edge with a stray thumb or finger (of either hand).

Table 1.1 Multitouch Gestures

To	Do This
Tap	Gently tap the screen with one finger.
Double-tap	Tap twice quickly. (If you tap too slowly, your iPad interprets it as two single taps.)
Touch and hold	Touch the screen with your finger, and maintain contact with the glass (typically, until some onscreen action happens).
Drag	Touch and hold a point on the screen and then slide your finger across the glass to a different part of the screen. A drag-like **slide** moves a control along a constrained path. You slide the iPad's brightness and volume sliders, for example.
Flick (or swipe)	Fluidly and decisively whip your finger across the screen. A faster flick scrolls the screen faster.
Pinch	Touch your thumb and index finger to the screen and then pinch them together (to zoom out) or spread them apart (to zoom in).
Rotate	Spread your thumb and index finger, touch them to the screen, and then rotate them clockwise or counterclockwise. (Or keep your fingers steady and rotate the iPad itself.)

Figure 1.2 Numbers in the App Store search results.

Getting Numbers

You can download Numbers from Apple's App Store, available on the iPad itself or from iTunes on your Mac or Windows PC. iCloud (page 126) automatically backs up the Numbers app and your spreadsheet files online, and copies Numbers to your other iOS devices (if you own more than one). To use the App Store and iCloud, your iPad must be connected to the internet and you must have an Apple ID (*appleid.apple.com*).

Tip: To sign in to, change, or create an Apple ID on your iPad, tap Settings > iTunes & App Store.

You can get Numbers from the iTunes App Store on your computer and then sync your iPad, but it's simpler and faster to download Numbers directly on your iPad. Tap the App Store icon on the Home screen, search for *iwork* (or *numbers*), find Numbers in the search results, and then download it (Figure 1.2). Numbers is free if you own a newer iPad; for older iPads, you must buy it.

Tip: Deleting Numbers also deletes your spreadsheets. To back them up to your computer, to a server, or to iCloud, see Chapter 7.

The Numbers Workspace

Numbers for iOS lacks the menus, toolbars, palettes, and advanced features of Numbers for Mac, but it provides a clean workspace suitable for tap-and-drag rather than point-and-click. This section provides an overview of the Numbers interface and workspace.

To open Numbers:

- Tap the Numbers icon on your Home screen.

    or

    Flick down on your Home screen to reveal the search field, type *numbers*, and then tap Numbers when it appears in the results list.

Tip: You can rotate your iPad to use Numbers in portrait (tall) or landscape (wide) view.

The spreadsheet manager

The first step in using Numbers is to create or open a spreadsheet to work on, which you do from the **spreadsheet manager** (Figure 1.3). This view is where Numbers lists all the spreadsheets that you've created or imported, and where you can open, rename, sort, copy, or delete them. Think of the spreadsheet manager as a "folder" for your existing spreadsheets as well as a starting point for new ones. See "Spreadsheets" on page 12.

To open the spreadsheet manager:

- If you're opening Numbers for the first time, tap through the introductory screens to open the spreadsheet manager.

    or

    If you don't see the spreadsheet manager, it means a spreadsheet is already open for editing; tap Spreadsheets in the top-left corner of the screen.

Create or import spreadsheets

Share, send, or convert spreadsheets

Create spreadsheet from template

Search for spreadsheets by name

Duplicate or delete spreadsheets

Toggle pop-up help tips

Sort spreadsheets

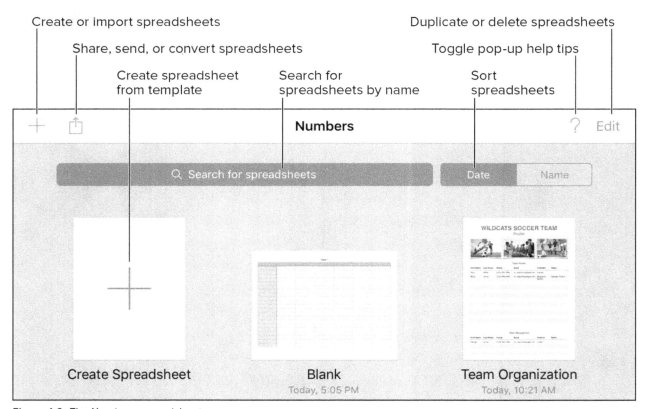

Figure 1.3 The Numbers spreadsheet manager.

Undo and Redo

Numbers stores your last few hundred actions, so you can undo and redo them. To undo your last change, tap Undo. To redo the last change that you undid, touch and hold Undo, and then tap Redo. To undo many changes, touch and hold Undo; the Undo menu will stay open while you tap Undo repeatedly. You can also shake your iPad to bring up the Undo/Redo dialog box. The iPad's accelerometer recognizes an intentional shaking motion—shaking front-to-back works better than shaking side-to-side. If you're typing, you can tap the undo or redo keys on the shortcut bar, the numbers-and-punctuation keyboard, or the symbols keyboard (see "Typing text" on page 35).

Numbers has no manual Save command—changes are saved automatically about every 30 seconds. If you make a mistake, use the Undo command.

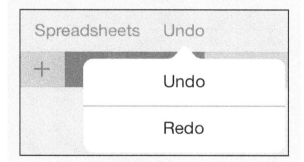

Viewing and editing spreadsheets

After you create a new spreadsheet or open an existing one in the spreadsheet manager, Numbers opens that spreadsheet for you to view or edit. Spreadsheets share a set of controls in the **toolbar** at the top of the screen (Figure 1.4).

Spreadsheets. Tap Spreadsheets to autosave your spreadsheet and return to the spreadsheet manager.

Undo/Redo. Tap (or touch and hold) to undo or redo your actions.

Sheet tabs. Sheets, which divide a spreadsheet into manageable groups, are shown as a row of tabs. To add a new sheet, tap + at the end of the tab bar. For details, see "Sheets" on page 20.

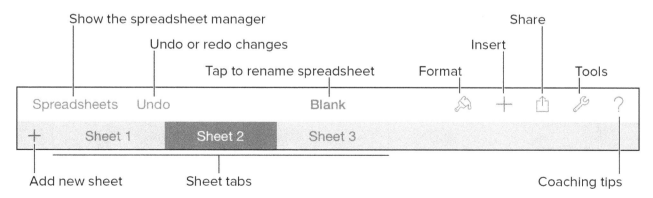

Figure 1.4 The Numbers toolbar.

Format menu. Tap 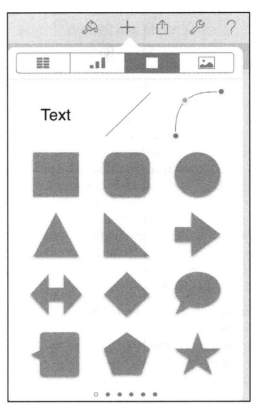 to view or change the attributes of tables, charts, photos, text boxes, and other spreadsheet objects. The options change depending on what you've selected (Figure 1.5). With a text box selected, for example, the menu displays a tabbed window that lets you change the box's style, text format, and layering. With a table cell selected, the menu lets you change the style, headers, and format of the table and its cells.

Insert menu. Tap + to add objects to your spreadsheet (Figure 1.6). **Objects** are the building blocks of spreadsheets—they're the design elements that you drag across a sheet's canvas to create your layout. Numbers objects include tables, charts, photos, videos, geometric shapes, and text boxes, which you can select, move, resize, rotate, copy, delete, layer, style, and manipulate by using the same basic techniques common to all iWork apps. Tap a symbol (media, tables, charts, text, or shapes) at the top of the + menu and then flick left or right within the menu to find a style you like. To add an object to your spreadsheet, tap it, or touch and hold and then drag it from the menu to the sheet.

Figure 1.6 The Insert menu.

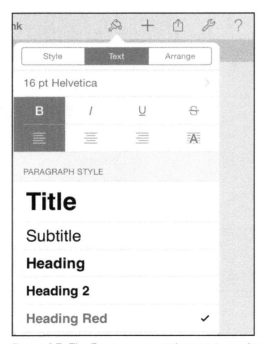

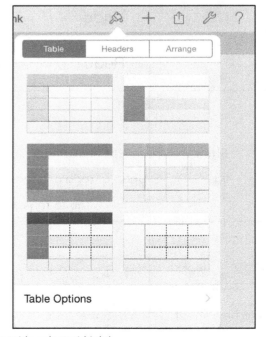

Figure 1.5 The Format menu with a text box selected (left) and a table selected (right).

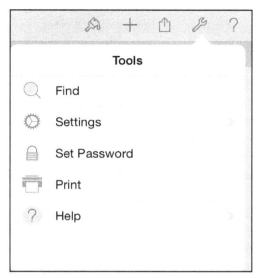

Figure 1.7 The Tools menu.

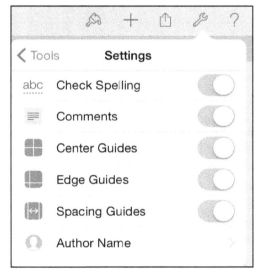

Figure 1.8 The Settings menu.

Tools menu. Tap to use Numbers's miscellaneous commands (Figure 1.7).

- **Find**. Search your spreadsheet for all instances of a particular word or phrase, and optionally replace each occurrence with new text. See "Using Editing Tools" on page 38.

- **Settings**. Check spelling, show or hide comments (and change your author name), or display **guides**, which are thin lines that appear temporarily to help you align objects as you resize them or drag them around the screen (Figure 1.8).

- **Set Password**. Password-protect (page 19) your spreadsheet.

- **Print**. Print spreadsheets (page 32) on a printer that you've set up to work with your iPad.

- **Help**. Launch Apple's searchable Numbers manual.

Share menu. Tap ⬆ to share or convert spread-sheets (Figure 1.9). For details, see Chapter 7.

Coaching tips. Tap ? to show or hide pop-up help tips (Figure 1.10).

Figure 1.9 The Share menu.

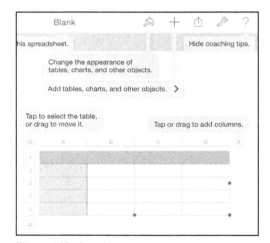

Figure 1.10 Coaching tips.

CHAPTER 2

Spreadsheet Basics

You'll need the skills covered in this chapter to create your spreadsheets, no matter how simple or complex. A Numbers spreadsheet provides a flexible, freeform canvas that you can use to enter and organize data; create tables and charts; manage lists; insert text, media, and graphics; and create formulas with more than 250 built-in functions and operators. If you've used other spreadsheet software, such as Numbers for Mac or Microsoft Excel, then many Numbers for iOS features will be familiar.

Spreadsheets

To get started with Numbers, launch it and either open an existing spreadsheet or create a new one based on one of the predesigned **templates**. Templates contain ready-made layouts, tables, charts, text boxes, and other elements—they're the quickest way to start a project because much of the work has been done for you. Exploring the different templates can show you how to assemble tables, charts, text, shapes, and photos into pleasing or professional-looking spreadsheets.

Figure 2.1 Newly created spreadsheets will appear in the spreadsheet manager.

- Each template is intended for a specific purpose (basic, personal, business, or education). Even if you don't use a template for its intended purpose, you still can choose it for its looks (color scheme, fonts, and formatting) and then delete its contents but not its style.

- To build your spreadsheet from scratch, use the Blank template.

- Editing a spreadsheet doesn't affect the template on which it's based.

- You can't edit or delete the built-in templates, but you can add custom templates.

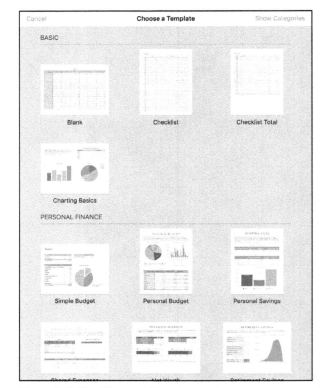

Figure 2.2 The Choose a Template screen.

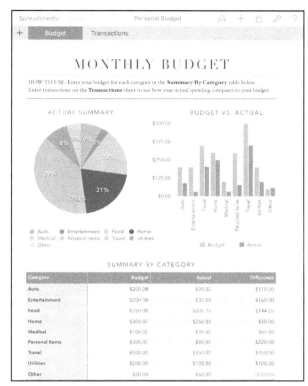

Figure 2.3 A new spreadsheet based on the chosen template.

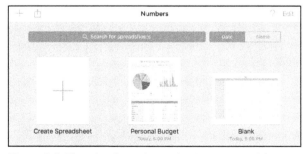

Figure 2.4 Thumbnail previews of existing spreadsheets in the spreadsheet manager.

To create a new spreadsheet:

1   In the spreadsheet manager, tap Create Spreadsheet (Figure 2.1). Alternatively, tap ┿ in the top-left corner and then tap Create Spreadsheet.

2   In the Choose a Template screen (Figure 2.2), flick up or down to see all the templates. The Blank template gives you a spreadsheet with only an empty table. The other templates contain a mix of tables, charts, placeholder text, photos, and other objects.

Tip: To see only certain types of templates, tap Show Categories in the top-right corner.

3   Tap the template that you want to use.

A new spreadsheet opens (Figure 2.3).

To open an existing spreadsheet:

■   Do any of the following:

▶   To open a local spreadsheet, in the spreadsheet manager (Figure 2.4), tap the thumbnail preview of the spreadsheet that you want to open. If necessary, flick up or down to the preview or tap the preview's folder. Each preview shows the spreadsheet's first sheet, name, and modification time.

▶   To open a spreadsheet stored in iCloud Drive, a third-party cloud location (such as Dropbox or Google Drive), a WebDAV server, or iTunes, tap ┿ in the toolbar in the top-left corner of the screen. For details, see "Moving Spreadsheets to the Cloud" on page 16 and Chapter 7.

▶   To open a spreadsheet sent via AirDrop (if available), flick up from the bottom of the screen to open Control Center, tap AirDrop, tap a discovery option, and then tap Add when the AirDrop message appears.

Tip: To open a copy of a spreadsheet to another (compatible) app, open the spreadsheet that you want to copy, tap ⬆ in the toolbar, and then tap Open in Another App.

To create a copy of a spreadsheet:

1   In the spreadsheet manager, locate the spread-
    sheet that you want to copy.

2   Tap Edit in the toolbar, or touch and hold the
    spreadsheet preview for a few seconds until all
    the previews wiggle.

3   Tap the preview of the spreadsheet that you
    want copy. To duplicate multiple spreadsheets
    at the same time, tap other previews to select
    additional spreadsheets.

    Selected spreadsheets have a heavy outline;
    tap again to deselect a selected spreadsheet
    (Figure 2.5).

4   Tap ⊞ in the toolbar. If you selected more than
    one spreadsheet, tap Duplicate Spreadsheets.

    All the selected spreadsheets are duplicated.

5   Tap Done in the toolbar.

To rename a spreadsheet:

1   In the spreadsheet manager, locate the preview
    of the spreadsheet that you want to rename.

2   Tap its name.

    A blinking insertion point appears.

3   Type a new name (Figure 2.6). You can double-
    tap the name to open a pop-up menu of editing
    commands, or drag across the text to move the
    insertion point.

4   When you're done typing, tap ⌨ or Done on
    the keyboard to dismiss the keyboard.

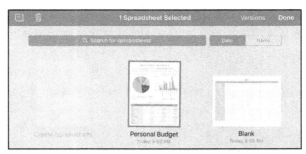

Figure 2.5 Selected spreadsheets have a heavy outline.

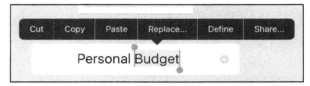

Figure 2.6 Double-tap the spreadsheet name to open a
menu of editing commands.

To delete a spreadsheet:

1 In the spreadsheet manager, locate the spreadsheet that you want to delete.

2 Tap Edit in the toolbar, or touch and hold the spreadsheet preview for a few seconds until all the previews wiggle.

3 Tap the preview of the spreadsheet that you want delete. To delete multiple spreadsheets at the same time, tap other previews to select additional spreadsheets.

   Selected spreadsheets have a heavy outline; tap again to deselect a selected spreadsheet.

4 Tap 🗑 in the toolbar, and then tap Delete Spreadsheet.

   All the selected spreadsheets are deleted.

Tip: You can't undo this action.

---

5 Tap Done in the toolbar.

To search for or sort spreadsheets:

1 In the spreadsheet manager, scroll down until the search field and sort buttons appear at the top of the view.

2 Type the name of a spreadsheet in the search field to find matches, tap Date to sort spreadsheets chronologically by their creation or modification time, or tap Name to sort spreadsheets alphabetically by file name..

Moving Spreadsheets to the Cloud

You can move a spreadsheet to a location on iCloud (page 126) or to a third-party cloud location that you've set up on your iPad (Dropbox or Google Drive, for example).

To move a spreadsheet:

1 In the spreadsheet manager, tap ⬆ and then tap Move To.

2 Tap the spreadsheet that you want to move.

3 Do any of the following:

- ▶ To move to the visible location, tap Move To This Location to place the spreadsheet outside a folder, or tap a folder and then tap Move to This Location.

- ▶ To move to another location, tap Locations, tap a service (iCloud or a third-party service), and then tap Move To.

- ▶ To move to a location that's not set up, tap Locations, tap More, tap the service to turn it on, and then tap Done. Tap the service (it now appears on the menu) and then tap Move To.

Tip: If you don't see a third-party service as an option, make sure that it's installed on your device. Free apps for Dropbox, Google Drive, and other cloud services are available in the App Store.

Handoff

When your Mac and iOS devices are near each other, you can use Handoff to pass a spreadsheet that you're working on from one to the other. You can start a spreadsheet on your iPad, for example, and then pick up where you left off on your Mac. Handoff requires:

- OS X 10.10 Yosemite or later on a Mac

- iOS 8 or later on an iOS device

- The same iCloud and Apple ID on both systems

- Bluetooth 4 (Bluetooth LE) on both systems

When Handoff is set up, a Handoff icon appears in the dock on your Mac, or in the bottom-left corner of your iOS device's lock screen. Set up Handoff in System Preferences on your Mac and in Settings on your iOS device. For details, read the Apple support article "Use Continuity to connect your iPhone, iPad, iPod touch, and Mac" at *support.apple.com/HT204681*.

Working with Earlier Versions of a Spreadsheet

Because Numbers saves your work continually, you can view earlier versions of a spreadsheet, save copies of earlier versions, or restore a spreadsheet to an earlier version.

To view, copy, or restore an earlier version of a spreadsheet:

1   In the spreadsheet manager, tap Edit in the toolbar.

All the spreadsheet previews wiggle.

2   Tap the preview of the target spreadsheet and then tap Versions in the toolbar.

The Version History window opens, listing earlier versions of the spreadsheet.

3   Tap an earlier version to select it and then do any of the following:

▸   To replace the current version with the earlier version, tap Restore. (The current version isn't deleted; it's saved as a previous version.)

▸   To leave the current version unchanged, tap Done.

▸   To view the earlier version, tap Preview. You can't edit the preview, but you can search for text, copy text and objects, close the preview, save a copy of the earlier version (leaving the current version unchanged), or restore the earlier version (replacing the current version).

Collaborators with editing privileges can copy and restore only the versions created after you shared the spreadsheet. Collaborators with view-only privileges have no access to earlier versions. See "Sharing spreadsheets via iCloud" on page 128.

If you add or change a spreadsheet password, the password applies only to versions created after the password was added or changed. To prevent others from restoring unprotected versions or versions with older passwords, stop sharing the spreadsheet, add a password to it, and then share the spreadsheet again. See "Password-protecting spreadsheets" on page 19.

Organizing spreadsheets into folders

If too many spreadsheets are crowding the spreadsheet manager, you can group them into **folders** to organize them compactly. It's a common practice to create multiple folders, each holding similar types of spreadsheets (personal, business, education, and so on). Folders save a lot of screen space and reduce excessive scrolling.

Tip: You can't create folders within folders.

To group spreadsheets into a folder:

1   In the spreadsheet manager, tap Edit in the toolbar, or touch and hold a spreadsheet preview for a few seconds until all the previews wiggle.

2   Tap to select multiple spreadsheets that you want to group into a single folder.

Selected spreadsheets have a heavy outline; tap again to deselect a selected spreadsheet.

If you want to create a folder containing only two spreadsheets, simply drag one spreadsheet onto another.

3   Touch and hold one of the selected spreadsheets until all the selected spreadsheets rise out of their positions in the grid, and then drag them onto another spreadsheet that you also want to include in the same folder (Figure 2.7).

A folder is created with all the spreadsheets contained within it.

4   Type a new name for the folder, if you like (Figure 2.8).

5   When you're done grouping spreadsheets, tap Done in the toolbar.

The folder appears in the spreadsheet manager.

6   Tap anywhere outside of the folder area to close it.

You can add more spreadsheets to an existing folder by dragging them onto it.

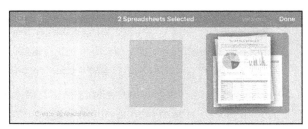

Figure 2.7 Drag spreadsheets to group them in a folder.

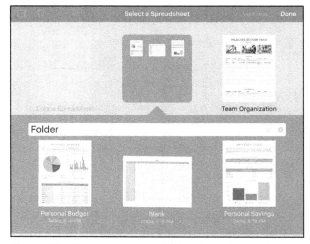

Figure 2.8 You can rename a folder at any time.

To remove spreadsheets from a folder:

1   In the spreadsheet manager, tap the folder to open it.

2   Tap Edit in the toolbar, or touch and hold a spreadsheet preview for a few seconds until all the previews wiggle.

3   Drag the spreadsheet anywhere onto the background, outside the folder.

4   Tap Done in the toolbar.

Password-protecting spreadsheets

To restrict access to a spreadsheet, set a password for it. Only those who know the password can open, read, or edit the spreadsheet. Password-protected spreadsheets are denoted by a lock symbol 🔒 in the toolbar and in the spreadsheet manager.

To assign a password to a spreadsheet:

- Tap 🔧, tap Set Password, type and retype the password, type an optional password hint (which everyone can see), and then tap Done.

  A password can consist of almost any combination of numbers, uppercase or lowercase letters, and keyboard symbols.

To change a password:

- Tap 🔧, tap Change Password, enter the requested information, and then tap Done.

To remove a password:

- Tap 🔧, tap Change Password, turn off Require Password, type the current password, and then tap Done.

Adding custom spreadsheet templates

To install a custom template on your iPad, save the template to iCloud, iTunes, a WebDAV server, or send it as an email attachment. Then, open it on your iPad. For details, see Chapter 7.

Tip: You can find third-party Numbers templates by searching the web or the App Store for *numbers templates* or *iwork templates*.

To install a custom template:

1 If you saved the custom template to iCloud, sync your iPad with iCloud.

  or

  If you copied it to a WebDAV server or attached it to an email, download the file to your iPad.

2 In the spreadsheet manager, tap the file (it has an identifying badge on it), and then tap Install.

  The template appears in the My Templates category in the Choose a Template screen.

To rename a custom template:

- In the spreadsheet manager, tap Create Spreadsheet, tap the custom template name, and then type the new name.

To delete a custom template:

- In the spreadsheet manager, tap Create Spreadsheet, touch and hold the template thumbnail, and then tap Delete.

Sheets

Sheets are tabs within a spreadsheet that divide information into logical groups. Each new sheet that you add is a blank canvas ready for tables, charts, text boxes, and other objects. For example, you can place tables of raw data on one sheet and charts, summary statistics, and conclusions on another. Or you can use sheets to segregate personal and business contacts. To get ideas for organizing sheets, browse the templates that came with Numbers.

Sheets are shown as a row of tabs at the top of the screen (Figure 2.9). Every new sheet is given a default name (Sheet 1, Sheet 2, and so on) that you can change to something more descriptive.

A sheet scrolls downward and to the right, beyond the last objects on it. Despite its name, don't think of a sheet as a single page; large sheets can span several pages when printed.

To add a new sheet:

- Tap + on the tab bar at the top of the screen, and then tap New Sheet in the pop-up menu (Figure 2.10).

    If you have no tables in your spreadsheet, tapping + will create a new sheet immediately, without showing you a pop-up menu. You can add as many sheets as you want within a spreadsheet.

To move from sheet to sheet:

- Flick or drag left or right to scroll the tabs along the top of the screen, and then tap a tab to activate its sheet.

    A bright-colored tab indicates the **active** (frontmost) sheet (Figure 2.11).

To rename a sheet:

- Double-tap the active sheet's tab at the top of the screen and then type a new name.

    Sheets within the same spreadsheet all must have different names. Numbers will cancel your edit if you type a duplicate name.

Figure 2.9 A row of sheet tabs.

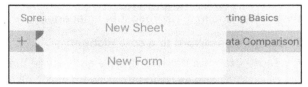

Figure 2.10 Tap + to add a new sheet to a spreadsheet.

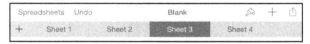

Figure 2.11 A colored tab indicates the active sheet.

Figure 2.12 Drag sheet tabs to reorder them.

Figure 2.13 Tap a tab to open the sheet menu.

Figure 2.14 The copy appears next to the original sheet.

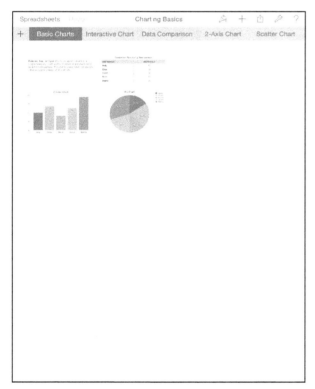

Figure 2.15 A zoomed-out sheet.

To reorder sheets:

- Touch and hold the sheet's tab until its color darkens slightly, and then drag it left or right to a new position in the tab bar (Figure 2.12).

    The other tabs slide to make way for the one you're dragging. If you want to move a sheet to a position that's not currently visible, drag its tab off the left or right edge of the screen to autoscroll the tabs.

    If you're moving a sheet a short distance, you can hold-and-flick (rather than hold-and-drag) its tab.

Tip: You can't move a sheet while you're renaming it (that is, while the insertion point is blinking within the tab's text). Tap outside the text.

To delete a sheet:

1   Tap the sheet's tab to activate it.

2   Tap the tab again, and then tap Delete in the pop-up menu (Figure 2.13).

    If the deleted sheet contains a table whose data are displayed as a chart in another sheet, then the links are severed and the chart reverts to a placeholder chart.

To make a copy of a sheet:

1   Tap the sheet's tab to activate it.

2   Tap the tab again, and then tap Duplicate in the pop-up menu.

    The copy appears alongside the original, with a slightly different name (Figure 2.14).

To zoom in or out on a sheet:

1   Tap the sheet's tab to activate it.

2   Touch two fingers to the sheet and then spread them apart (to zoom in) or pinch them together (to zoom out) (Figure 2.15).

    As you zoom, a pop-up indicator shows the current magnification level, which ranges from 50% to 200%. Zooming is continuous but snaps into place at the 100% and 150% levels.

Tables

A **table** is a grid of rows and columns used to organize, analyze, and present data. At each row–column intersection is a **cell**, which holds an individual
data value: a number, text, a date, the result of a
formula, and so on. Every table has a name that
optionally can be displayed above the table. You
can change the default names (Table 1, Table 2, and
so on) to something more descriptive.

Tables typically are where you spend most of your
time when building a spreadsheet. You can add as
many tables as you like to a spreadsheet, though
it's common to have spreadsheets where a single
table is the only object.

To add a table to a sheet:

1 Tap the sheet's tab to activate it.

2 Tap ➕ in the toolbar and then tap ▦ (Figure
   2.16).

   To see the available table styles, flick right or left
   in the ▦ menu. The styles are preset to match
   the template you're working in.

3 Tap the table style that's closest to what you
   want to use (Figure 2.17).

   A new, empty table appears on the sheet with a
   preset number of rows and columns. Whatever
   the look of the table you begin with, you can
   customize it.

To select a table:

■ Tap the table and then tap ◎ in the top-left
   corner of the table (Figure 2.18).

To move a table on a sheet:

1 Tap the table to select it.

2 Drag ◎ in the top-left corner of the table to
   position the table on the sheet.

Figure 2.16 The Tables menu.

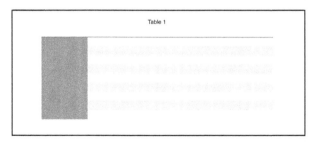

Figure 2.17 A new, empty table appears on the sheet.

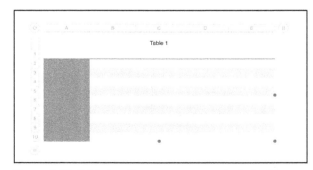

Figure 2.18 Table handles appear on a selected table.

Figure 2.19 As you resize a table, edge guides appear.

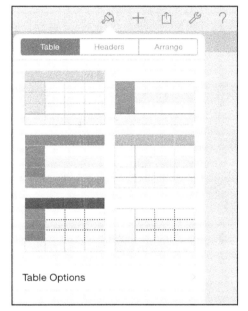

Figure 2.20 The Table menu.

Figure 2.21 The Table Options menu.

To resize a table:

1 Tap the table to select it.

2 Tap ⊙ in the top-left corner of the table and then drag one of the blue selection handles ● on the table's perimeter (Figure 2.19).

As you resize the table, edge guides appear to help you align the table with other objects. A pop-up label shows the dimensions of the resized table.

To change the style of a table:

1 Tap the table to select it.

2 Tap 🖌 in the toolbar, and then tap Table.

3 To change the color scheme, tap a table style in the Table menu (Figure 2.20).

Changing a table's color scheme won't change its structure; the table keeps the same number of rows, columns, headers, and footers.

4 To show or hide the table name, table outline (border), alternating row colors, or grid lines, or to adjust fonts, tap Table Options at the bottom of the Table menu and then set your preferences in the Table Options menu (Figure 2.21).

You may need to flick up or down in a menu to see all its options (the Table Font list, for example, is quite long). When you're done, tap off the menu or, to backtrack to other options, tap ⟨ at the top of the menu.

To cut, copy, or delete a table:

1   Tap the table to select it.

2   Tap ⊙ in the top-left corner of the table and then tap Cut, Copy, or Delete in the pop-up menu (Figure 2.22).

Cut removes the table so that it can be moved (pasted) elsewhere. Copy copies a table so that it can be duplicated (pasted) elsewhere, leaving the original table intact. Delete clears the table and all its data. To paste a cut or copied table, go to the destination (which can be in the same sheet or in a different sheet or spreadsheet), tap an empty area on the sheet, and then tap Paste in the pop-up menu.

To rename a table:

1   Tap the table to select it.

2   If necessary, show the table name: tap 🖌 > Table > Table Options > Table Name > On, and then tap the table again to reselect it.

3   Double-tap the table name.

A blinking insertion point appears.

4   Type a new name.

You can double-tap the table name to open a pop-up menu of editing commands (Figure 2.23). To format the name, select a range of text and then tap 🖌.

5   When you're done typing, tap ⌨ or Done on the keyboard to dismiss the keyboard.

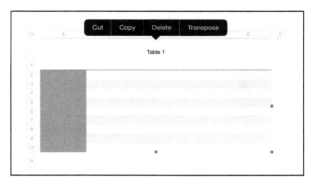

Figure 2.22 The table menu.

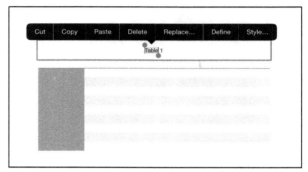

Figure 2.23 You can use standard editing commands to change a table's name.

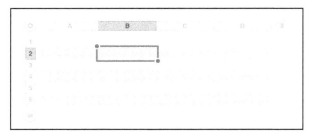

Figure 2.24 A selected cell.

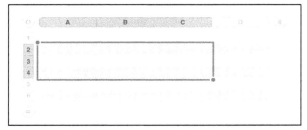

Figure 2.25 A range of selected cells.

Cells

A cell is an individual box within a table that can hold a data value and is identified by the intersection of its row and column. This section shows the basics of selecting cells. (To edit the contents of cells, see Chapter 3.)

To select a cell:

- Tap the cell.

    A heavy border with blue selection handles ● surrounds a selected cell (Figure 2.24). (Selection handles won't appear when the onscreen keyboard is open. Tap ⌨ or Done on the keyboard to dismiss the keyboard.)

To select a range of cells:

1 Tap any cell in the range.

2 Drag the blue selection handles ● in any direction (up, down, left, right, or diagonally) to encompass the cells that you want to select (Figure 2.25).

    You can release the selection handles and then drag them again to change the selected range. Dragging a selection handle near the edge of the screen autoscrolls the selection in the direction of the drag.

Rows and Columns

You can add, delete, select, resize, and rearrange the rows and columns of a table. A table's overall size changes as you add or delete rows or columns.

Selecting rows and columns

When you select a row or column, you can manage masses of data easily—move or copy the selection to a new location in the table, delete the whole row or column, format or style all the cells in the selection, and more.

To select entire rows or columns:

1 Tap the table to select it.

   The table handles appear.

2 Tap the bar to the left of the row or above the column that you want to select.

   The entire row or column is selected.

3 To extend the selection, drag the blue selection handles ● to encompass the rows or columns that you want to select (Figure 2.26 and Figure 2.27).

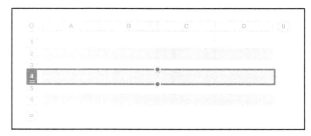

Figure 2.26 A selected row in a table.

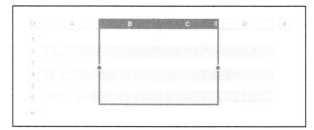

Figure 2.27 Selected columns in a table.

Adding and deleting rows and columns

If you have other tables or objects on the sheet, Numbers nudges them relative to the resized table, preventing the table from colliding with those objects when it gets larger, or from creating too much space between objects when it gets smaller.

To add or delete columns:

1 Tap the table to select it.

   The table handles appear.

2 Do any of the following:

   ▶ To add columns on the right side of the table, drag ⑪ rightward.

   ▶ To delete empty columns on the right side of the table, drag ⑪ leftward. (You can't delete non-empty columns by using this method.)

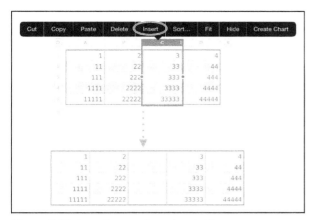

Figure 2.28 Inserting a column in a table.

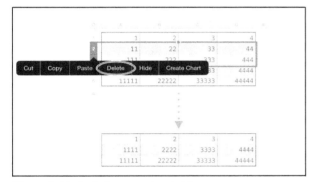

Figure 2.29 Deleting rows in a table.

▸ To add a column anywhere in the table, select a column, and then tap Insert in the pop-up menu (Figure 2.28). (If you select multiple columns, the Insert command doesn't appear.) A column is inserted to the left of the column that you selected. If you're adding a leftmost column, tap an option to specify whether you want it to be a body or header column.

▸ To delete columns anywhere in the table (including non-empty columns), select a column or range of columns, and then tap Delete in the pop-up menu.

To add or delete rows:

1 Tap the table to select it.

The table handles appear.

2 Do any of the following:

▸ To add rows to the bottom of the table, drag ⊜ downward.

▸ To delete empty rows at the bottom of the table, drag ⊜ upward. (You can't delete non-empty rows by using this method.)

▸ To add a row anywhere in the table, select a row, and then tap Insert in the pop-up menu. (If you select multiple rows, the Insert command doesn't appear.) A row is inserted above the row that you selected. If you're adding a topmost or bottommost row, tap an option to specify whether you want it to be a body, header, or footer row.

▸ To delete rows anywhere in the table (including non-empty rows), select a row or range of rows, and then tap Delete in the pop-up menu (Figure 2.29).

Copying and moving rows and columns

To cut, copy, or paste rows or columns:

1 Tap the table to select it.

   The table handles appear.

2 Select the desired rows or columns, tap the blue part of the bar adjacent to the selection, and then tap a command in the pop-up menu (Figure 2.30).

To move rows or columns by dragging:

1 Tap the table to select it.

   The table handles appear.

2 Select the rows or columns that you want to move, touch and hold the blue part of the bar adjacent to the selection until the selection rises out of the table, and then drag to a new position in the table (Figure 2.31).

   As you drag the selection, existing rows or columns slide out of the way. (You can't use this method to overwrite data, as you would with cut, copy, and paste.)

Resizing rows and columns

To resize rows or columns:

1 Tap the table to select it.

   The table handles appear.

2 Select the row(s) or column(s) that you want to resize. If you select a range of rows or columns, they'll all be resized to the same height or width.

3 Do any of the following:

   ▶ To resize rows, drag the bottom edge of the blue bar ▤ on the left of a selected row upward or downward (Figure 2.32).

   ▶ To resize columns, drag the right edge of the blue bar ▮ above a selected column leftward or rightward.

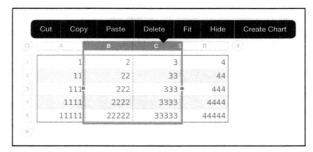

Figure 2.30 The column pop-up menu.

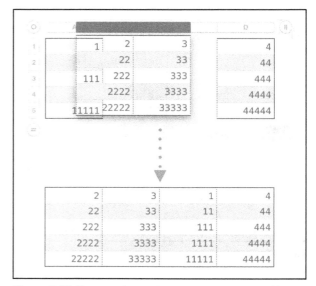

Figure 2.31 You can drag columns or rows to move them.

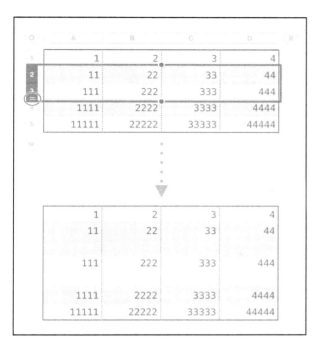

Figure 2.32 Resizing rows in a table.

To autofit rows or columns to the size of the tallest or widest entry:

1 Tap the table to select it.

   The table handles appear.

2 Select the row(s) or column(s) that you want to resize. If you select a range of rows or columns, they'll all be resized.

3 Tap the blue part of the bar adjacent to the selection and then tap Fit in the pop-up menu.

To hide rows or columns:

1 Tap the table to select it.

   The table handles appear.

2 Select the row(s) or column(s) that you want to hide. If you select a range of rows or columns, they'll all be hidden.

3 Tap the blue part of the bar adjacent to the selection and then tap Hide in the pop-up menu.

Tip: Think of hidden rows or columns as having a row height or column width of zero.

To unhide (show) all rows and columns in a table:

1 Tap the table to select it.

   The table handles appear.

2 Tap ⊙ in the top-left corner of the table and then tap Unhide All in the pop-up menu.

   Use this technique if you import a table that contains hidden rows and columns.

Tip: To unhide only rows or only columns, select any row or column and then tap Unhide Rows or Unhide Columns in the pop-up menu.

Adding and deleting headers and footers

You can label your table data by designating **header rows and columns**, which are formatted to stand out from the actual data (the **body rows and columns**). Header rows are anchored directly above the topmost body row, with their cells labeling the columns below. Header columns are directly to the left of the leftmost body column, with their cells labeling the rows to the right. When you print a table, its headers appear on each page, making long tables easier to read. You can keep the data labels in view by **freezing** header rows or columns. When you scroll through a table, frozen headers remain visible at the edge of the table, floating above the rest of the table.

You can use **footer rows** when you want to draw attention to the bottom rows of a table. Footer rows are formatted so that they stand out from the other (body) rows and typically are used to call out sums and averages under columns of numbers.

To add or delete header rows, header columns, or footer rows:

1   Tap the table to select it.

The table handles appear.

2   Tap 🖌 in the toolbar, and then tap Headers (Figure 2.33).

3   Tap the header and footer –/+ buttons for the items that you want to adjust (Figure 2.34). Existing rows or columns are converted to headers or footers. You can add as many headers as the table will allow, as long as at least one body row and column remains. The color scheme changes automatically to highlight the headers and footers.

When a table has both header rows and header columns, they share cells where they intersect in the top-left corner of the table. Those shared cells are considered to be part of the header row.

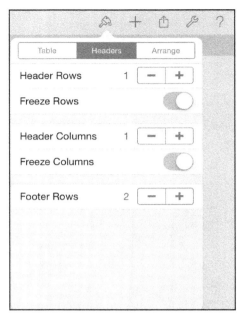

Figure 2.33 The Headers menu.

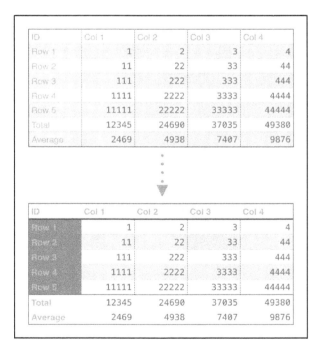

Figure 2.34 A table with headers and footers.

	Q1	Q2	Q3	Q4
Product 1	$180	$150	$220	$240
Product 2	$140	$150	$150	$170
Product 3	$90	$200	$140	$130

	Product 1	Product 2	Product 3
Q1	$180	$140	$90
Q2	$150	$150	$200
Q3	$220	$150	$140
Q4	$240	$170	$130

Figure 2.35 A table and its transpose.

Transposing rows and columns

You can transpose the rows and columns in a table to swap them—row 1 becomes column A (the contents of row 1 move into column A) and vice versa, row 2 becomes column B, and so on.

To transpose rows and columns:

1 Tap the table to select it.

2 Tap ⊙ in the top-left corner of the table and then tap Transpose in the pop-up menu (Figure 2.35).

The results of transposing are:

- Rows and columns resize to the default width and height for the table.

- Header rows become header columns and footer rows become the rightmost columns.

- The table style presets and manual style changes are preserved, including alternating row colors, grid lines, table and cell outlines, cell and text styles, hidden rows and columns, and so on.

- Chart data references update.

- Merged cells transpose normally, unless they're in the header row. In some cases, transposing unmerges merged header row cells.

- If the transposed table isn't a valid form, sort and filter rules are discarded and the form is unlinked.

- Warnings flag any formulas that can't be updated after transposing.

Tip: To revert all the changes, select the table and then transpose it again. This operation undoes the previous transposing.

Printing Spreadsheets

You can print Numbers spreadsheets wirelessly from an **AirPrint**-capable printer that you've set up to work with your iPad. To set up a printer, read the Apple support article "About AirPrint" at *support. apple.com/ht201311*.

If you don't have an AirPrint-capable printer, an easy way to print your spreadsheet is to transfer it to your computer by using one of the methods covered in Chapter 7 and then print it from there. You can also use a third-party cloud-storage app such as Dropbox or Google Drive to transfer the spreadsheet wirelessly to your computer.

Unless the target computer can open native Numbers files, you should transfer spreadsheets in PDF or Excel (.xlsx) format. The target computer should have the same fonts installed that you used in the spreadsheet (even for PDF transfers, which don't contain embedded fonts).

A few third-party apps provide iPad-based printing by getting a spreadsheet from an app and sending it to a printer—either directly to a shared network printer or wirelessly via a helper program that you install on your computer. To find a printing app, search for *print* or *printer* in the App Store. The easiest way to print from these apps is to email a PDF copy of a spreadsheet to yourself and then open it by using the Open In menu in Mail (for details, see "Sending Copies of Spreadsheets" on page 122).

To print a spreadsheet from an AirPrint-capable printer:

1   Open the spreadsheet, tap 🔧 in the toolbar, and then tap Print.

2   In the Print Preview screen (Figure 2.36), select formatting and layout options. The onscreen preview shows what the final printout will look like.

3   Tap Print in the lower-right corner of the screen.

4   In the Printer Options window (Figure 2.37), select the printer, the range of pages to print, the number of copies, and any other options that your printer supports (such as double-sided output).

5   Tap Print in the Printer Options window.

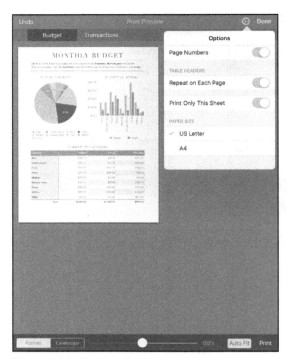

Figure 2.36 The Print Preview screen.

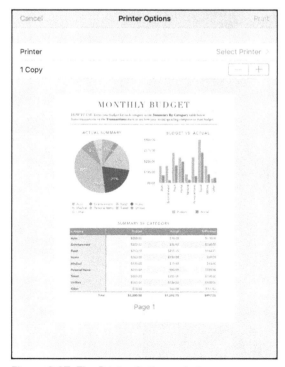

Figure 2.37 The Printer Options window.

CHAPTER 3

Entering Data

The first task in building a spreadsheet is to enter your raw data into table cells. Each cell holds an individual value: a number, text, a date, or a duration. (Formulas, which are mathematical and functional expressions that resolve to values, are covered in Chapter 4.) Numbers provides specialized on-screen keyboards that pop up when you edit a cell's contents. You can also do the usual operations common to many spreadsheets: copy and move cells, fill series of values, edit lists via data-entry forms, and sort rows. This chapter describes how to work with cells and their contents.

Tip: To import your data rather than typing it directly into Numbers, see Chapter 7.

Editing Cells

A virtual keyboard appears onscreen whenever you tap any editable area (Figure 3.1). Keyboards reorient for portrait (tall) and landscape (wide) views. Typing is straightforward and works the same way as typing in other apps.

You enter different types of data by using Numbers' different keyboards, accessed by tapping the buttons on the left side of the formula bar (above the keyboard). Tap ㊷ to enter numbers, 🕐 to enter dates, times, and durations, ⓣ to enter text, or ⊜ to enter formulas. If you're editing a formula, you can tap ⚫ to show the buttons for the other keyboards.

To edit the contents of a cell:

- Double-tap the cell and then use the keyboard to type your data (Figure 3.2).

To move from cell to cell when editing cell contents:

- To move to the cell to the right of the current cell, tap ➡ on the keyboard (if you're in the last cell of a row, a column is added).

  To move to the first cell below the current cell or row, tap ⬅ (if you're in the last cell of a column, a row is added).

Tip: The ➡ and ⬅ keys don't appear on the text keyboard ⓣ.

To delete the contents of cells:

- Select a cell or a range of cells, tap the selection, and then tap Delete in the pop-up menu (Figure 3.3).

Figure 3.1 The text keyboard in Numbers.

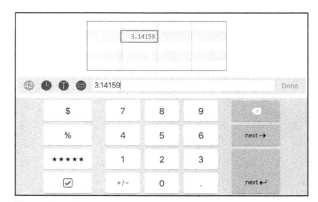

Figure 3.2 Editing a cell.

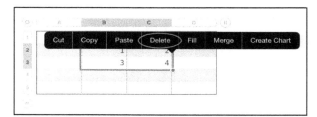

Figure 3.3 Deleting the contents of cells.

Figure 3.4 Touch and hold a key to see its character variants.

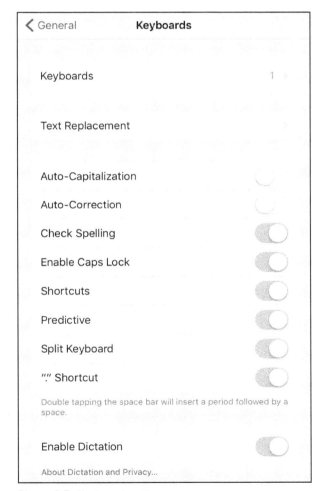

Figure 3.5 Keyboard settings.

Typing text

The text keyboard lets you type text in table cells, text boxes, and shapes. Numbers has three types of text keyboards 🅣: alphabetic, numbers-and-punctuation, and symbols keyboards.

- You can touch and hold certain keys to see variants of their characters in a pop-up display. The E key, for example, lets you type not only the standard e but also ë, é, è, ê, and other diacritics (Figure 3.4).

- In the alphabetic keyboard, tap the .?123 key to see numbers and most punctuation; within that layout, tap the #+= key to see less-common symbols, tap 123 to return to the numbers-and-punctuation layout, or tap ABC to return to the alphabetic keys.

- A quick way to type a character on the numbers-and-punctuation or symbols keyboard is to touch and hold the .?123 or #+= key and (still touching the screen) slide your finger up to the character that you want, and then lift your finger. (Characters are typed only when you lift your finger.)

- To delete the last character that you typed, tap ⌫.

- To dismiss the keyboard, tap ⌨ or Done, or tap outside of the onscreen keyboard.

- To adjust keyboard behavior, on your Home screen, tap Settings > General > Keyboard (Figure 3.5).

- You can use an external (physical) keyboard with Numbers. To use a wireless keyboard, on your Home screen, tap Settings > Bluetooth, and then pair your keyboard and iPad.

Tip: You can dictate text on an iPad 3 or newer or an iPhone 4S or newer (iOS 5 or later required).

Selecting and editing text

The basic text-editing operations are:

- **Select** highlights text to edit, cut, copy, or format.

- **Cut and paste** removes (cuts) content and places it in the clipboard so that it can be moved (pasted) elsewhere. Cutting deletes the content and formatting from its original location.

- **Copy and paste** copies content to the clipboard so that it can be duplicated (pasted) elsewhere. Copying leaves the original content and formatting intact (nothing visible happens).

Tip: The select, cut, copy, and paste operations also apply to tables, rows, columns, cells, charts, photos, text boxes, shapes, and other objects.

You can select any portion of text within a cell, text box, or shape, and then edit it by typing or by using the standard cut, copy, and paste operations:

- When you tap text in an editable area, a blinking **insertion point** indicates where new text will appear when you type or paste.

- Numbers' templates contain **text placeholders**. Double-tap a placeholder to replace its text with your own.

- To move the insertion point, touch and hold near where you want to place it until a magnifying glass appears, and then drag over the text to the new position and lift your finger (Figure 3.6).

- You can flick left or right to move the insertion point through text quickly. Flick across a paragraph with one finger to move the insertion point one character in the direction of the flick. Flick with two fingers to move to the beginning or end of the current word. Flick with three fingers to move to the beginning or end of the current line.

- To select a word, double-tap it. To select a paragraph, triple-tap it (or single-tap it with two fingers). Alternatively, double-tap a word and then, without lifting your finger, drag to encompass the range that you want to select, including whole or partial words and paragraphs.

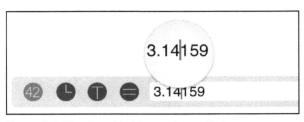

Figure 3.6 Touch and hold text to magnify it.

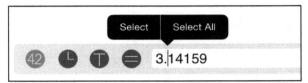

Figure 3.7 The pop-up menu for the insertion point.

Selecting Text Quickly

On iOS 9 or later, you can use the onscreen keyboard as a trackpad to select text quickly.

- To move the insertion point, touch the keyboard with two fingers, maintaining contact with the glass. The keyboard darkens and all the keys turn blank. Drag both fingers anywhere on the screen and then lift them when the insertion point is where you want it.

- To select text, move the insertion point to where you want the selection to begin (or end), and then double-tap the keyboard with two fingers, maintaining contact with the glass. The nearest word is selected. Drag both fingers to extend the selection.

In some editing contexts, you can touch or double-tap two fingers anywhere on the screen, not only on the keyboard.

Tip: These features are easier to use if you spread both fingers slightly before touching the screen.

Figure 3.8 Drag the blue handles to change the selection.

Figure 3.9 The pop-up menu for selected text.

Hyperlinks

When you type or paste a web address (URL) or email address in a text box or shape (but not a table), Numbers recognizes it and autoformats it as an underlined **hyperlink**. (The link must be followed by a space or punctuation mark for Numbers to recognize it.) To open the link or copy its URL to the clipboard (for later pasting), tap the link to make a pop-up window appear, and then tap Open (for web addresses), New Message (for email addresses), or Copy. Tapping Open switches to Safari or Mail. To edit or remove the link, tap Link Settings.

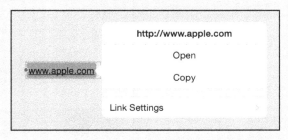

- To open the selection pop-up menu, tap once in an editable area, and then tap again in the same place (Figure 3.7). The Select command selects the current word. The Select All command selects all the text (or all the objects in the sheet, if you've tapped on an empty area of the sheet).

- To extend or shorten the range of selected text, select a word and then drag the blue selection handles ● to encompass the characters or paragraphs that you want to select (Figure 3.8). When you drag beyond the edge of the current paragraph, the selection changes to contain the entire paragraph; you can drag the selection handles up or down to select multiple paragraphs (flick to exit paragraph selection).

- To cut or copy text, select a range of text, tap Cut or Copy, and then move the insertion point (or select some text to replace) and tap Paste (Figure 3.9).

- Buttons on the **shortcut bar** (above the keyboard) provide quick, context-sensitive access to common commands such as bold, italic, copy, paste, and undo. To toggle shortcuts, on the Home screen, tap Settings > General > Keyboard > Shortcuts.

- Numbers has no manual Save command—changes are saved automatically about every 30 seconds. If you make a mistake, use the Undo command in the top-left corner of the screen.

The Clipboard

The **clipboard** is the invisible area of memory where Numbers stores cut or copied content, where it remains until it's overwritten when you cut or copy something else. This scheme lets you paste the same thing multiple times in different places. You can transfer content from Numbers to another program—such as Keynote or Pages—provided that program can read content generated by Numbers. Note that you can't paste something that you've deleted (as opposed to cut), because Numbers doesn't place deleted content in the clipboard.

Using Editing Tools

You can find every instance of a word or phrase in your spreadsheet and optionally change it to something else. You can also find and correct misspellings, and look up words in the built-in dictionary.

To find or replace text:

1. Tap 🔧 in the toolbar and then tap Find.

2. In the search field, type the text that you want to find. You can tap in the field to show a pop-up menu of the standard editing commands (cut, copy, paste, and so on).

   All instances of matching text are highlighted in the sheet; the current instance is selected and highlighted in yellow (Figure 3.10).

3. If you want to constrain the search results, tap ⚙ and then turn on Match Case or Whole Words.

4. If you want to replace the found text with new text, tap ⚙, tap Find and Replace, and then type the new text in the Replace field.

5. Do any of the following:

   ▸ To find the next or previous instance of the text, tap 〉 or 〈.

   ▸ To replace the current instance of the text, tap Replace.

   ▸ To replace all instances of the text, touch and hold Replace, and then tap Replace All.

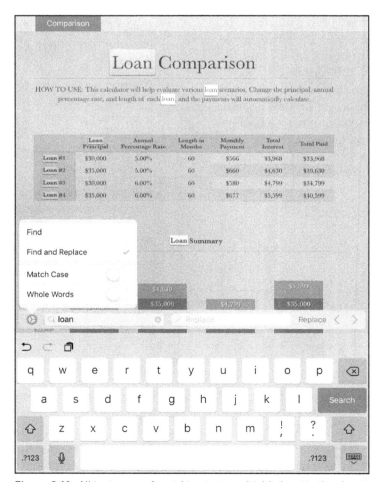

Figure 3.10 All instances of matching text are highlighted in the sheet.

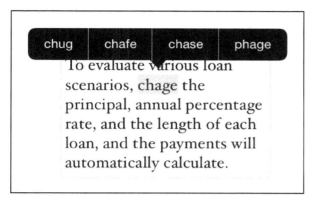

Figure 3.11 Tap a misspelled word for suggestions.

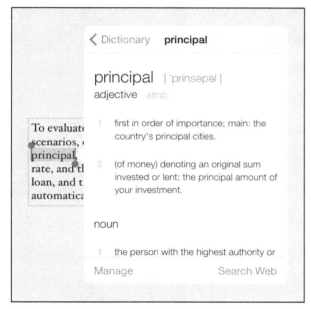

Figure 3.12 The dictionary window.

To find and correct misspellings:

1   Tap in the toolbar, tap Settings, and then turn on Check Spelling.

Numbers underlines misspelled words in red. If spelling suggestions don't appear automatically, double-tap a word, and then tap Replace in the pop-up menu.

2   To correct a misspelled word, tap it, and then tap one of the suggested spellings in the pop-up menu (Figure 3.11). The spelling dictionary recognizes some proper names.

To look up a word in the dictionary:

■   Double-tap the word and then tap Define in the pop-up menu.

The definition appears in the pop-up dictionary window (Figure 3.12). Flick up or down in the window to see the entire entry. You don't have to be connected to the internet to use the dictionary.

Adding Comments and Highlights

Adding **comments** and text **highlighting** to your work lets you make personal notes, query reviewers or collaborators, insert editorial or proofreading suggestions, and so on. Anyone who can access the spreadsheet can add comments to text, objects, charts, table cells, and the spreadsheet itself. Commented text is highlighted with a color unique to the comment's author. Objects and table cells with comments have a comment marker □ . If you don't want to see comments and highlights, you can hide them.

To add, read, or delete comments:

- Do any of the following:

  ▶ To add a comment, select text or tap an object or table cell, and then tap Comment in the pop-up menu. Type your comment, and then tap outside the comment to finish.

  ▶ To read a comment, tap its comment marker □ . To go to the next or preceding comment, tap > or < in the comment (Figure 3.13).

  ▶ To delete a comment, tap its comment marker □ , and then tap Delete in the comment.

  ▶ To add a comment directly to the spreadsheet, tap an empty area on a sheet, and then tap Comment in the pop-up menu. These comments are always open. You can move a spreadsheet comment by dragging its title bar or resize it by dragging its bottom-right corner.

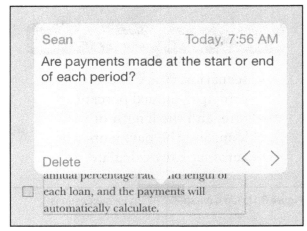

Figure 3.13 A snippet of commented and highlighted text.

To set the author name:

- Tap ✎ in the toolbar, tap Settings, tap Author Name, and then type a name.

To highlight text:

- Select the text, and then tap Highlight in the pop-up menu.

  To remove the highlight, select or tap the text, and then tap Remove Highlight in the pop-up menu.

Tip: You can add a comment to highlighted text: tap the highlighted text, and then tap Comment in the pop-up menu.

To show or hide comments:

- Tap ✎ in the toolbar, tap Settings, and then turn on or off Comments.

Formatting and Styling Cells

You can apply a format to a cell to display its value in a particular way. Applying a currency format, for example, displays a currency symbol (such as $, £, €, or ¥) in front of numbers in cells. To make a cell stand out, you can change its style (typeface, color, alignment, border, and so on). Cell formats and styles determine only how cell values are displayed; the data aren't affected.

You can format empty cells. When you enter a value in the cell, it's displayed using the cell's format. Clearing a cell (backspacing over its contents) removes its value but not its formatting; deleting the contents (tapping Delete in the pop-up menu) removes both.

A formatted cell automatically displays the correct keyboard for its data type. The buttons in the left column of the numeric keyboard offer a quick way to change formats.

To format cells:

1 Select a cell or a range of cells to format.

2 Tap 🖌 in the toolbar, and then tap Format (Figure 3.14).

3 To apply a default format quickly, tap a format name in the Format list.

   or

   To set options for a format, tap ⓘ next to a name in the Format list and then set the cell format options described in "Cell format options" on page 44.

   Cell values update instantly to reflect the formatting options that you choose.

   The three columns in Figure 3.15 show the same value of a number, a date, and a duration, respectively, but formatted differently. When a cell is used in a formula, its actual value is used, not its formatted value.

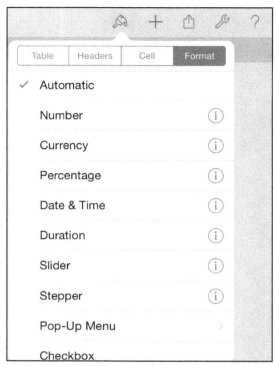

Figure 3.14 The Format menu.

1.5	Nov 5, 2012	1w 3d 12h
1.500	11/5/2012 12:00 AM	1 week 3 days 12 hours
1.50E+00	Mon, Nov 5, 2012	1:3:12
1 1/2	11/5/2012	1w 4d
$1.50	5-Nov-2012	10 days 12 hours
€ 1.5000	5-Nov	252h
150.0%	Nov-12	11 days

Figure 3.15 Examples of formatted cells.

Figure 3.16 The Cell menu.

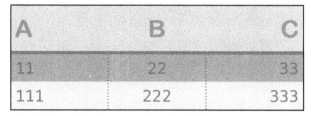

Figure 3.17 Examples of styled cells.

To style cells:

1 Select a cell or a range of cells to style.

2 Tap ✎ in the toolbar, and then tap Cell (Figure 3.16).

3 Do any of the following:

- ▶ Tap a typeface button to apply bold, italic, underline, or strikethrough.

- ▶ Tap Text Options to set the text size, text color, and font.

- ▶ Tap the top alignment buttons to align text horizontally within the cell: left, center, right, or justified. The bottom alignment buttons align text vertically within the cell: top, middle, or bottom.

- ▶ Tap Fill Color to choose a background color (flick left or right in the color menu to see all the colors).

- ▶ Tap Border Style to put a border around the cells.

- ▶ Tap Wrap Text in Cell to set whether a value in a cell can spill into adjacent, empty cells.

Cell values update instantly to reflect the style options that you choose (Figure 3.17).

Cell format options

When table cells are selected, the 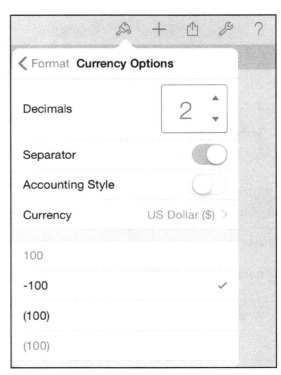 > Format menu lets you choose from among the following formats. You can tap ⓘ next to a format name to set specific options.

- **Automatic**. Tap Automatic to let Numbers choose a format based on cell contents.

- **Number**. Tap Number for standard number formatting (Figure 3.18). Tap the arrows to set the number of decimal places. Tap Separator to show or hide thousands separators. Tap an option to set the appearance of negative values. Tap Scientific to make numbers appear in scientific notation. Tap Fraction to make numbers appear with a numerator and denominator.

- **Currency**. Tap the arrows to set the number of decimal places (Figure 3.19). Tap Separator to show or hide thousands separators. Tap Accounting Style to position the currency symbol. Tap Currency to select a currency symbol. Tap an option to set the appearance of negative values.

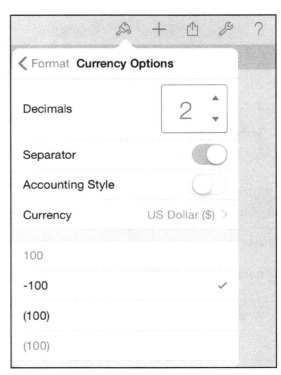

Figure 3.19 The Currency Options menu.

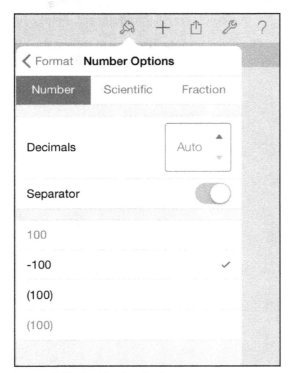

Figure 3.18 The Number Options menu.

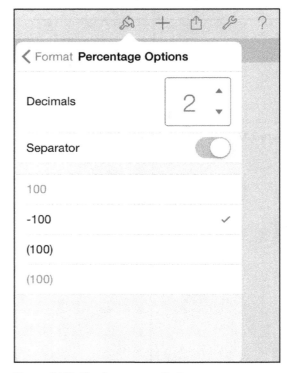

Figure 3.20 The Percentage Options menu.

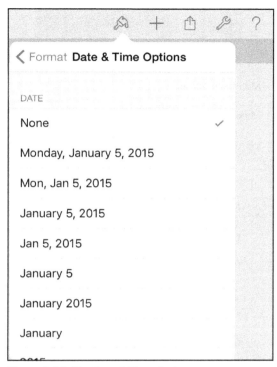

Figure 3.21 The Date & Time Options menu.

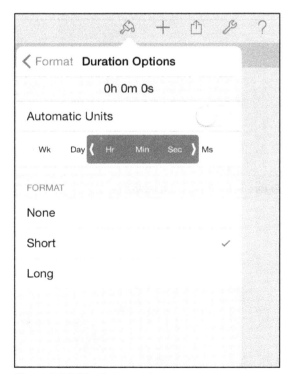

Figure 3.22 The Duration Options menu.

- **Percentage**. Tap the arrows to set the number of decimal places (Figure 3.20). Tap Separator to show or hide the thousands separators. Tap an option to set the appearance of negative values.

- **Date & Time**. Tap the Date format and the Time format that you want (Figure 3.21). Flick up or down in the menu to see all the options.

- **Duration**. To manually specify which time units appear, turn off Automatic Units (Figure 3.22). Drag the left or right end of the duration range selector to encompass the scale of the time duration that you want to use, from weeks (Wk) to milliseconds (Ms). Under Format, select None to display no time units, Short to display time units as abbreviations, or Long to spell out the entire time units.

- **Slider.** A **slider** constrains a cell's number, currency, or percentage value to a range that you specify. To set the value in the cell, drag the slider (Figure 3.23 and Figure 3.24).

  Tap Minimum Value to set the start of the slider's range (for example, type *0* (zero) to limit cell values to values greater than or equal to zero). Tap Maximum Value to set the end of the slider's range (for example, type *100* to limit cell values to values less or equal to 100). Tap Increment to set the number of units that you want each stopping point on the slider to represent (for example, type *0.5* to allow half units to be entered into the cell, or type *1* if you want only whole units to be entered). Tap Number, Currency, or Percentage to format the cells' contents.

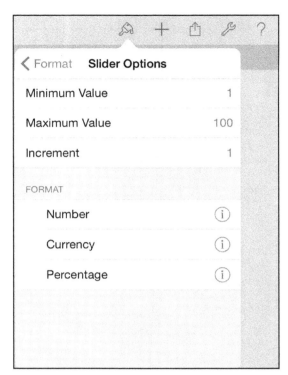

Figure 3.23 The Slider Options menu.

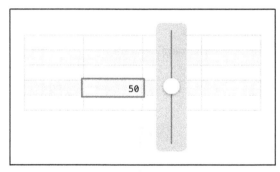

Figure 3.24 A slider example.

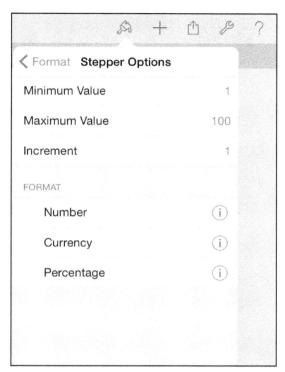

Figure 3.25 The Stepper Options menu.

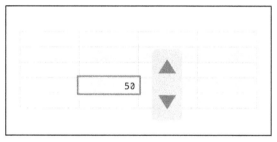

Figure 3.26 A stepper example.

- **Stepper**. A **stepper** constrains a cell's number, currency, or percentage value to a range that you specify. To increase or decrease the value in the cell, tap the up or down arrows (Figure 3.25 and Figure 3.26).

  Tap Minimum Value to set the start of the stepper's range (for example, type *0* (zero) to limit cell values to values greater than or equal to zero). Tap Maximum Value to set the end of the stepper's range (for example, type *100* to limit cell values to values less or equal to 100). Tap Increment to set the number of units that you want each stopping point on the stepper to represent (for example, type *0.5* to allow half units to be entered into the cell, or type *1* if you want only whole units to be entered). Tap Number, Currency, or Percentage to format the cells' contents.

- **Pop-Up Menu**. A **pop-up menu** constrain a cell's value to an item in a list of options that you specify. To enter a value into the cell, choose an item from the pop-up menu (Figure 3.27 and Figure 3.28).

  The initial state of the Pop-Up Options window depends on the contents of the selected cell(s). If the selected cell(s) are empty, the items in the window are empty (*Item 1*, and so on, appear as placeholder text). If the selected cell(s) contain values, the items in the window are prefilled with those values. Up to 100 unique values are allowed. Checkboxes are interpreted as *true* or *false* text, and star ratings are assigned their numerical value between 0 and 5. The pop-up menu selection in each cell matches that cell's original value.

  ▶ To add a menu item, tap Next in the keyboard, or tap ⊕ or "add new item", and then type the item text.

  ▶ To delete a menu item, tap ⊖, and then tap Delete.

  ▶ To reorder menu items, drag ≡.

  ▶ To display the first item in the pop-up menu as the default entry for cells in which no item has been chosen from the pop-up menu, tap First Item.

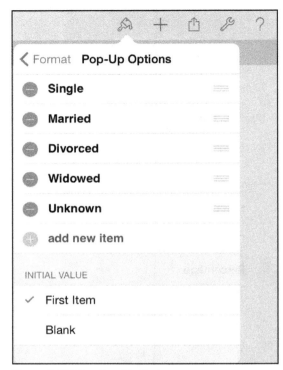

Figure 3.27 The Pop-Up Options menu.

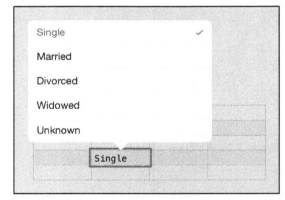

Figure 3.28 A pop-up menu example.

- **Checkbox**. A **checkbox** indicates one of two states: yes or no, on or off, complete or incomplete, for or against, alive or dead, and so on. These **boolean values**, as programmers call them, are a simple choice of TRUE or FALSE. In Numbers, you use checkboxes to toggle a cell's value between TRUE (✓, checked) and FALSE (, unchecked). To toggle the value of a checkbox, double-tap the cell to edit it, and then either tap the cell again or tap ✓ **true** or ☑ **false** in the formula bar. The built-in Checklist template shows a common use for checkboxes: a to-do list.

Tip: In mathematical formulas and sorting operations, the checkbox value of TRUE is 1 (one) and FALSE is 0 (zero). If you sum a column of checkboxes, for example, the result is the number of checkboxes that are checked. It's also common to multiply by a checkbox to force the result to be zero if the box is unchecked.

- **Star Rating**. A **star rating** displays the integers 0–5 as a number of star symbols; to change a star rating, tap a star or dot (or double-tap the cell and then tap ★ ★ ★ ★ ★ in the formula bar). Star ratings, like checkboxes, can be used in mathematical formulas and sorting operations.

- **Text**. Use the Text format for alphanumeric text.

Removing cell controls

You can remove the controls from table cells and return them to the state of empty, unformatted cells, or you can convert them to a different kind of cell format.

To remove or convert controls in cells:

1 Select the target cell(s).

   If you're deleting the control from a cell that contains a slider, stepper, pop-up menu, checkbox, or star rating, touch and hold a cell you want to edit, and then adjust the selection to include all the target cells.

2 To remove all content from the cells, tap the selected cells again, and then tap Delete in the pop-up menu.

   or

   To convert the existing cell values from one type to another, tap ⟐ in the toolbar, tap Format, and then tap another cell format type. If cells containing pop-up menus are converted to Text format, they retain their contents as static text. Slider and stepper cells converted to Number format retain their values as static numbers. Some data types can't be converted (for example, you can't convert a list of text items in a pop-up menu to Number format). If you try to convert to an incompatible cell format, the cell controls aren't removed from the cell.

Cutting, Copying, and Pasting Cells

You can cut or copy cells and paste them within the same table, to another table, or to an empty area on a sheet to create a new table. You can also paste cells to a different spreadsheet file—the contents of the clipboard don't change when you close one spreadsheet and open another.

For an overview of cut, copy, and paste, see "Selecting and editing text" on page 36. If your data range contains formulas, you're given the option of pasting the formulas or only their computed values; see also "Copying and Moving Formulas" on page 78.

To cut, copy, and paste cells:

1   Select the range of cells that you want to cut or copy.

2   Tap the selection, and then tap Cut or Copy in the pop-up menu (Figure 3.29).

3   Select the destination cell(s), tap the selection, and then tap Paste. Numbers replaces the values and formatting of the destination cells. The destination determines how Numbers pastes the clipboard contents:

   ▸   When you select only one destination cell, Numbers pastes the entire clipboard, using that cell as the top-left corner of the pasted cells (Figure 3.30).

   ▸   When the selected destination has the *same* dimensions (that is, the same number of rows and columns) as the clipboard's contents, Numbers pastes the entire clipboard unchanged (Figure 3.31).

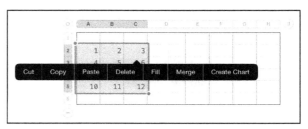

Figure 3.29 The Cut, Copy, and Paste commands.

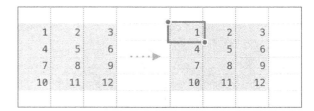

Figure 3.30 Pasting to a one-cell destination.

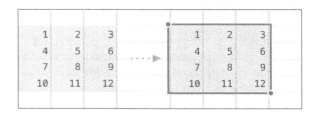

Figure 3.31 Pasting to a same-sized destination.

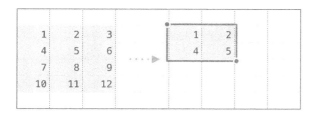

Figure 3.32 Pasting to a smaller destination.

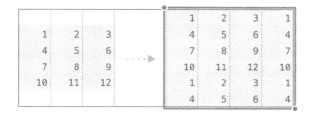

Figure 3.33 Pasting to a larger destination.

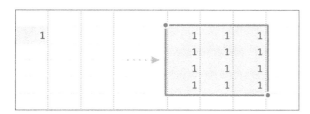

Figure 3.34 Pasting a single cell to a larger destination.

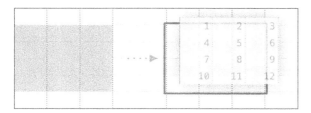

Figure 3.35 Dragging cells to a destination.

▶ When the selected destination has *smaller* dimensions than the clipboard's contents, Numbers pastes only a subset of the clipboard, starting with the top-left corner (Figure 3.32).

▶ When the selected destination has *larger* dimensions than the clipboard's contents, Numbers pastes the entire clipboard, repeating rows and columns to fill the entire destination (Figure 3.33).

▶ Pasting a single cell to a range of cells clones the original cell in every cell of the destination (Figure 3.34).

▶ To add the cells to a sheet as a new table, tap an empty area of the sheet, tap again, and then tap Paste.

To move cells by dragging:

1 Select the range of cells that you want to move.

2 Touch and hold the selection until it rises out of the table.

3 Drag it to another location in the same table (Figure 3.35).

A transparent image of the original cells follows your drag. Numbers highlights the cells where the selection will land when you lift your finger. (You can't drag to another table or to an empty area of the sheet.)

Merging Cells

Merging table cells combines adjacent cells into one, removing the borders so that they behave as a single cell.

Merged cells are treated specially in formulas (Chapter 4):

- To refer to a merged cell in a formula, use the address of the merged cell's top-left corner.

- You can't include only part of a merged cell in a cell range that's used in a formula.

- You can include merged cells within cell ranges used in formulas only if the entire cell is included within the range.

- If you refer to a cell in a formula, and then merge it with cells that are outside the formula's intended range, then the formula may return an error (page 82).

Tip: If you've already created a form (page 56) to enter data into a table, then you can't merge any of the cells in that table.

To merge cells:

1   Select a range of two or more cells (Figure 3.36).

2   Tap the selection, and then tap Merge in the pop-up menu.

    The cells are merged (Figure 3.37). If only one cell contained a value before merging, the merged cell retains the value and formatting of that cell. If multiple cells contained values before merging, all the values are retained but converted to text formatting. If any cells have a fill color, the merged cell takes on the fill color that was in the top-left cell.

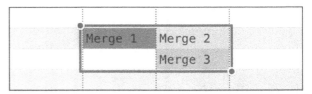

Figure 3.36 Cells before merging.

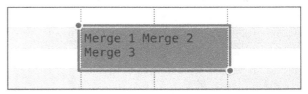

Figure 3.37 Merged cell.

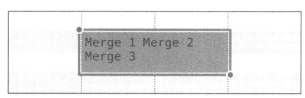

Figure 3.38 Cell before unmerging.

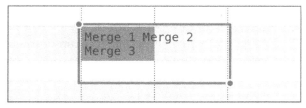

Figure 3.39 Unmerged cells.

To unmerge cells:

1 Select a merged cell (Figure 3.38).

2 Tap the selection, and then tap Unmerge in the pop-up menu.

The merged cell's original values are retained in the top-left cell (Figure 3.39).

Filling Cells with Data Series

Fill creates a column or row of values based on just one or two cells that Numbers can extrapolate into a series. Fill looks at the values that you've already entered in a row or column and infers the additional values to add. Fill recognizes standard data series:

- Numbers that regularly increase (1, 2, 3) or decrease (–5, –10, –15)

- Letters (A, B, C)

- Days (Sunday, Monday, Tuesday) and months (Jan, Feb, Mar), either written out or in three-letter abbreviations

- Alphanumeric serial numbers, where text is followed by digits (ABC-01, ABC-02, ABC-03)

You can also use fill to copy a single cell multiple times (like a fast copy-and-paste). If you select one cell that contains a number or text that's not part of a standard series, fill will copy that value to all the target cells in the row or column.

If you start with three or more cells with an irregular interval, fill simply repeats the pattern; selecting three cells containing 8, 2, and 13, for example, fills the target cells with 8, 2, 13, 8, 2, 13, … .

Fill doesn't establish an ongoing relationship among cells. After filling, you can change the cells in the filled range independently. When you fill a formula into new cells, Numbers updates the formula's cell references to reflect the new locations. For details, see "Copying and Moving Formulas" on page 78.

Figure 3.42 shows before-and-after results of filling columns with different starting values. Note the series in column 5—filling decimal (floating-point) numbers can lead to unexpected results due to rounding.

To fill a range of cells:

1 Enter the starting value(s) of the series in a row or column.

2 Select the cell(s) that you just entered.

3 Tap the selection, and then tap Fill in the pop-up menu (Figure 3.40).

   A yellow box appears around the cell(s).

4 Drag a side of the yellow box along the row or column that you want to fill. You can drag up or down along the same column or left or right along the same row, but you can't drag diagonally to fill a block of cells.

   Numbers fills the row or column with the next values in the series (Figure 3.41). If any target cells already contain data, Numbers overwrites them with the new values and formats.

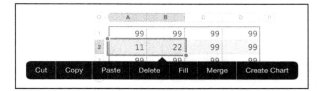

Figure 3.40 Tap Fill in the pop-up menu.

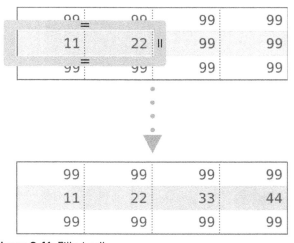

Figure 3.41 Filled cells.

1	10	2	0.0	1.33	1	Feb	Monday	S	Item 0	A-5
	11	-2	1.5	1.66	1		Wednesday			A-10
					2					
					3					

1	10	2	0.0	1.33	1	Feb	Monday	S	Item 0	A-5
1	11	-2	1.5	1.66	1	Mar	Wednesday	T	Item 1	A-10
1	12	-6	3.0	1.99	2	Apr	Friday	U	Item 2	A-15
1	13	-10	4.5	2.32	3	May	Sunday	V	Item 3	A-20
1	14	-14	6.0	2.65	1	Jun	Tuesday	W	Item 4	A-25
1	15	-18	7.5	2.98	1	Jul	Thursday	X	Item 5	A-30
1	16	-22	9.0	3.31	2	Aug	Saturday	Y	Item 6	A-35
1	17	-26	10.5	3.64	3	Sep	Monday	Z	Item 7	A-40
1	18	-30	12.0	3.97	1	Oct	Wednesday	A	Item 8	A-45
1	19	-34	13.5	4.30	1	Nov	Friday	B	Item 9	A-50

Figure 3.42 Examples of filled cells.

Using Forms to Edit Lists

A **form** is a view of a table (a special sheet) designed for quick data entry. When you link a table to a form, Numbers automatically updates each row in the table as you enter information on the form—each table row is shown as a single page on the form. If you make any changes to the table directly, such as editing cells, adding or deleting columns, or changing data types, the form self-updates to match those changes. Forms work best with large tables, when it would be cumbersome to navigate rows, read across columns, and edit data directly in the table. The built-in template named Attendance shows an example of a table and form.

To create and use a form:

1 Make sure that the table for which you want to create a form has a header row (Figure 3.43). A header column is optional. For details, see "Adding and deleting headers and footers" on page 30.

2 Tap + on the tab bar at top of the screen, and then tap New Form in the pop-up menu.

3 Tap the name of the source table in the list of tables.

4 In the form that appears (Figure 3.44), the name of the linked table is shown on the form's sheet tab. The indicator in the form's top-right corner shows the current row number and total number of rows. If the table has a header column, its (editable) values appear above the data-entry grid rather than in it. Do any of the following:

   ▶ To edit a value, tap it.

   ▶ To go to the next or preceding row in the table, tap > or <.

   ▶ To navigate rows quickly, drag up or down the dots along the right side of the screen.

   ▶ To add a new row after the current row, tap ✛.

   ▶ To delete the current row, tap 🗑.

   ▶ Flick up and down the form to see all its fields.

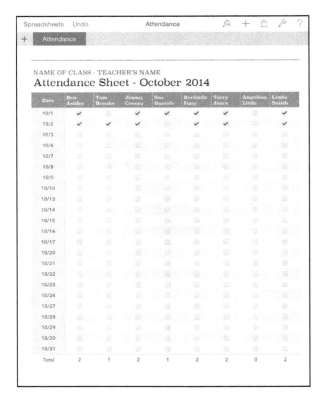

Figure 3.43 A source table (with header row) for a form.

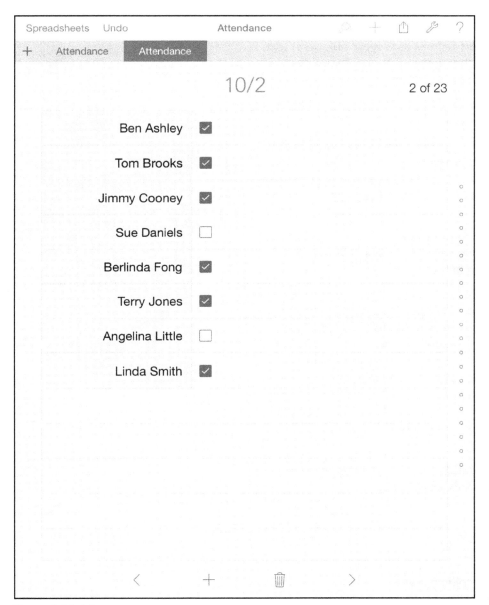

+   Attendance   Attendance

10/2

Ben Ashley ☑

Tom Brooks ☑

Jimmy Cooney ☑

Sue Daniels ☐

Berlinda Fong ☑

Terry Jones ☑

Angelina Little ☐

Linda Smith ☑

Figure 3.44 A form.

Sorting Rows in a Table

You can order the rows in a table, making values easier to find and patterns easier to spot.

- You can sort in ascending order (A, B, C...1, 2, 3...Jan, Feb, Mar) or descending order (Z, Y, X...3, 2, 1...Dec, Nov, Oct).

- You can sort on any data type: numbers, text, dates, checkboxes, and so on. For text values, sorting is case-sensitive.

- Rows are ordered according to the values in a specified column.

- Entire rows stay intact when they jump to their new sorted positions in the table. Sorting on a column doesn't mean that you're sorting only that column—rows always keep all their column values.

- Header and footer rows (page 30) don't move when a table is sorted; they stay fixed at the top and bottom of the table.

- Unlike Numbers for Mac and Microsoft Excel, Numbers for iOS doesn't support multi-column sorts, which are used to break ties when two or more rows have the same value in a sort column. But there's a workaround: to do a multi-column sort on the columns A, B, and C, for example, work backward: first sort on column C, then B, and then A. This technique works because Numbers retains the order of rows when sorting tied values.

- Numbers for iOS doesn't support filtering (hiding certain categories of rows).

To sort rows:

1 Tap the table to select it.

   The table handles appear.

2 Select the column that you want to sort on, and then tap Sort in the pop-up menu (Figure 3.45).

3 Choose whether to sort in ascending or descending order.

   Numbers sorts the rows of the table (Figure 3.46).

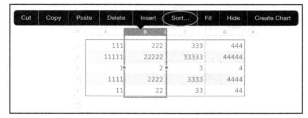

Figure 3.45 An unsorted table.

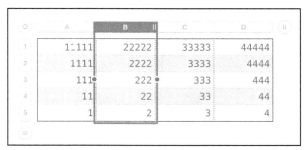

Figure 3.46 A sorted table.

CHAPTER 4

Formulas and Functions

After you enter and organize your data values in tables, you can use formulas and functions to transform raw numbers to meaningful information. A **formula** performs a calculation and displays the result in the cell where you enter the formula, called a **formula cell**. Formulas can do things as simple as adding two numbers, but functions are the real power of spreadsheets. **Functions** are built-in, named operations, such as SUM and AVERAGE, that perform a wide range of calculations for statistics, probability, dates and times, finance, engineering, text, and more.

Formula Essentials

A formula cell displays the result of its calculation and, on the surface, looks like any other (nonformula) cell. By just looking at a table, you can't tell the difference between a cell that contains a formula whose result is 3 and a cell that contains the number 3 (the number typed in directly). It's crucial to distinguish a formula's two display components: the formula itself and the resulting value. The actual contents of a formula cell is an equation—the formula—that tells Numbers how to generate that cell's value. It's that value, and not the formula, that's used in any calculations that refer to the cell.

- You enter each formula into a single cell. A formula can **reference** other cells on the spreadsheet, but the entire formula itself resides only in the cell where its result is displayed.

- Numbers recalculates the result of a formula every time you open a spreadsheet or change a data value that the formula uses. In Figure 4.1, for example, if you change any Test 1 score, Numbers auto-updates the values of the formula cells showing that column's average, maximum, and minimum. For small tables or simple formulas, updates occur instantly; for large tables or complex formulas, updates are slower.

- Formulas can operate on and display results in any data type: numbers, text, dates, times, durations, or boolean (true/false) values.

Calculating Random Numbers

Numbers for iOS lacks Excel's Calculate Now (F9) feature, so you must use a clunky workaround to force the RAND and RANDBETWEEN functions to return a different random value when the spreadsheet recalculates. Here's one way: format any cell as a checkbox (page 44). In the cell where you want the random number to appear, enter the formula

```
=IF(cell-ref, RAND(), RAND())
```

where *cell-ref* refers to the checkbox cell. Repeatedly turn on and off the checkbox to force recalculation of RAND.

To view a formula:

- Double-tap the cell containing the formula.

    Numbers opens the formula keyboard and displays the cell's formula in the **formula bar** above the keyboard. The formula bar lets you view, as well as edit, formulas. The table in Figure 4.1 shows students' test scores. The selected cell in the second column (cell address B7) shows the average score of all five students on the first test. The formula bar shows the actual contents of the cell (which uses the AVERAGE function), and the cell itself displays the formula's result (81).

Figure 4.1 The formula bar lets you view and edit formulas.

Parts of a Formula

Every formula uses some combination of the following elements (Figure 4.2).

Equal sign (=). The formula keyboard auto-enters the equal sign required at the start of every formula; you can't forget or delete it.

Constants. Constants, also called literals or static values, are numbers, text, dates, times, durations, or boolean (true/false) values. Constants never change unless you edit them explicitly in a formula.

Arithmetic operators. These operators do basic math. The **unary arithmetic operators** work on only one numeric value (Table 4.1). The **binary arithmetic operators** work on two numeric values (Table 4.2).

Cell references. These references point to the cell or range of cells whose values you need to do a calculation. See "Cell References" on page 67.

Comparison operators. These operators compare two values and return a boolean (true/false) value depending on their relationship (equal, not equal, less than, and so on). See "Comparison Operators" on page 72.

Functions. Functions built into Numbers let you do a wide range of calculations. The TODAY function, for example, returns today's date, and STDEV calculates the sample standard deviation of a range of numbers. See "Functions" on page 74.

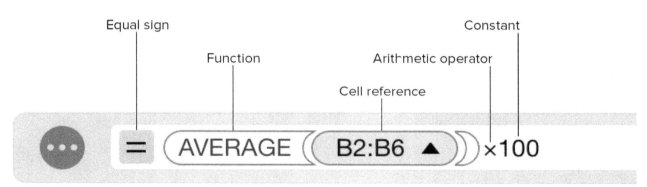

Figure 4.2 The parts of a formula.

Table 4.1 Unary Arithmetic Operators

Operator	Description	Example	Result
−	The **negation operator** reverses the sign (positive or negative) of a value	8 + −2	6
+	The **identity operator** leaves a value unchanged (rarely useful)	8 − +2	6
%	The **percent operator** divides a value by 100	2%	0.02 (formatted as 2%)

Table 4.2 Binary Arithmetic Operators

Operator	Description	Example	Result
+	The **addition operator** adds two values	2 + 4	6
−	The **subtraction operator** subtracts the second value from the first	2 − 4	−2
×	The **multiplication operator** multiplies two values	2 × 4	8
÷	The **division operator** divides first value by the second	2 ÷ 4	0.5
^	The **exponentiation operator** raises the first value to the power of the second	2 ^ 4	16

Entering Formulas

The simplest type of formula sets a cell value equal to a constant, but typing =2 is no different than just typing 2 in a cell—no formula needed. Nontrivial formulas use operators and functions. The formula =1+1 uses the addition operator to sum two constants. The leading equal sign, supplied for you when you use the formula keyboard, distinguishes a formula from text, numbers, dates, and other raw values. When entering a formula, you can use most of the standard editing techniques described in "Editing Cells" on page 34.

The formula bar always displays the complete formula. You must type formulas on the formula keyboard ⊜. If you use the text keyboard ⊕ and type =1+1, Numbers treats the entry as text and displays =1+1 instead of calculating the result. Tapping ⦁⦁⦁ on the formula bar shows buttons that open Numbers' other (nonformula) keyboards.

To enter a formula in a cell:

1   Double-tap the cell.

2   If you're entering a new formula, tap ⊜ on the left side of the formula bar (just above the keyboard) to open the formula keyboard.

    or

    If you're editing an existing formula, the formula keyboard opens automatically.

3   Position the insertion point in the formula bar or select an element to change or replace, and then do any of the following (Figure 4.3):

    ▶   To insert a constant, type it. For numbers, tap the numeric keys on the formula keyboard. For text, tap the "abc" key. For dates, times, and durations, tap the 🕒 key. For boolean values, tap the true/false key (tap it repeatedly to toggle the value).

    ▶   To insert an arithmetic operator, tap its key on the left side of the formula keyboard. If the arithmetic operators aren't visible because the comparison operators are showing, tap the ()+÷ key.

    ▶   To insert a cell reference, see "Cell References" on page 67.

    ▶   To insert a comparison operator, see "Comparison Operators" on page 72.

    ▶   To insert a function, see "Functions" on page 74.

    ▶   To remove an element, select it or position the insertion point to the right of the element, and then tap ⊗. To remove multiple elements, you can tap repeatedly or touch and hold ⊗.

4   When you're done, tap ✓ to enter the formula, or tap ✕ to cancel and revert to the cell's previous contents.

Saving Formulas

Instead of tapping ✓ to save your formula and dismiss the keyboard, you can move from cell to cell and enter more formulas. To move to the cell to the right of the current cell, tap ➡ on the keyboard (if you're in the last cell of a row, a column is added). To move to the first cell below the current cell or row, tap ↵ (if you're in the last cell of a column, a row is added).

When you finish editing a formula, don't tap another cell to save the formula. Recall from "Editing Cells" on page 34 that, normally, when you edit a cell's contents, tapping any other cell will save your changes and select the tapped cell. When you're editing a formula in the formula bar, however, tapping another cell inserts a reference to that cell in the formula itself.

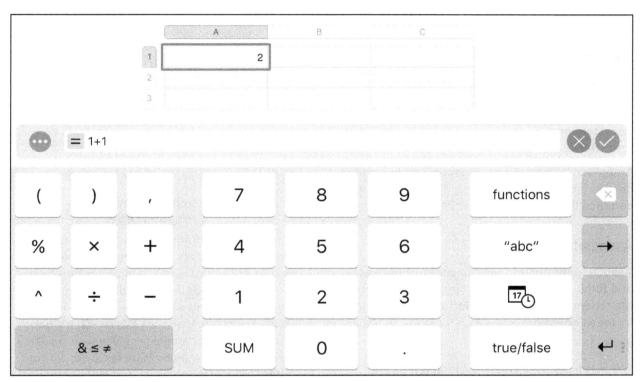

Figure 4.3 Entering a formula.

Evaluation Order

Numbers uses rules of precedence and associativity to determine the order in which it evaluates each part of an arithmetic formula.

Precedence

Precedence determines the priority of various operators when more than one operator is used in a formula. Operations with higher precedence are performed first. The formula

=2+3×4

is 14 rather than 20 because multiplication has higher precedence than addition. Numbers first calculates 3×4 and then adds 2.

Operators with lower precedence are less **binding** than those with higher precedence. Table 4.3 lists operator precedences from most to least binding; operators in the same row of the list have equal precedence.

Arithmetic operators have higher precedence than comparison operators (page 72) but lower precedence than functions (page 74).

Associativity

Associativity determines the order of evaluation in a formula when adjacent operators have equal precedence. Numbers uses left-to-right associativity for all operators, so

=6÷2×3

is 9 (not 1) because 6÷2 is evaluated first, and

=2^3^2

is 64 (not 512) because 2^3 is evaluated first.

Table 4.3 Order of Evaluation (Highest to Lowest)

Operator	Description
()	Calculations inside parentheses
−, +, %	Unary negation, unary identity, unary percent
^	Exponentiation
×, ÷	Multiplication, division
+, −	Addition, subtraction

Using Parentheses to Control Evaluation Order

You can use parentheses to override precedence and associativity rules. Expressions inside parentheses are evaluated before expressions outside them. Adding parentheses to the preceding examples, you get (2+3)×4 is 20, 6÷(2×3) is 1, and 2^(3^2) is 512. It's good practice to add parentheses (even when they're unnecessary) to lengthy formulas to ensure your intended evaluation order and make formulas easier to read.

=5^2×4÷2

is equivalent to

=((5^2)×4)÷2

but the latter is clearer.

Use parentheses in pairs (one closing parenthesis for every opening one). If you mismatch parentheses, Numbers flags a syntax error (page 82) in your formula.

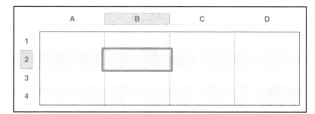

Figure 4.4 Cell-reference tabs.

Cell References

The real power of formulas comes from using cell references to identify (point to) cells whose values you want to use.

Cell reference basics

The letters and numbers on a table's **reference tabs** identify the columns and rows, respectively. Reference-tab letters refer to columns. Reference-tab numbers refer to rows. In Figure 4.4, cell B2 is selected.

Each **cell reference** is an address named for the column–row intersection where the cell is located. B2, for example, is the cell at the intersection of column B and row 2. A range of cells is identified by a pair of cell references separated by a colon (:). A1:B3, for example, refers to the rectangular block of six cells between A1 and B3 inclusive—that is, cells A1, A2, A3, B1, B2, and B3.

The first 26 columns of a table are labeled from A to Z. Column 27 is labeled AA, column 28 is AB, and so on. Cell BC500, for example, is located at the intersection of column 55 and row 500.

A cell reference in a formula tells Numbers to get that cell's value and use it in the formula's calculation. The simplest example is

=A1

which sets the value of the formula cell to whatever value is in cell A1. You can treat cell references like ordinary values. The formula

=A1×2

returns twice the value of A1, provided that A1 holds a number.

The formula in Figure 4.5 references multiple cells. The formula cell, C3, sums the values in the four cells A1, B1, A2, and B2, which are temporarily color-coded to match the colors used in the formula bar. Formulas always reflect the current state of the spreadsheet. If you change any value in the range A1:B2, Numbers recalculates the result in C3 automatically.

Cell reference formats

Cells are also referenced by name by using header-column and header-row values (page 30). If cell B4 has the header-column value Qtr1 and the header-row value Div33, its named reference is Qtr1 Div33.

Referenced cells can be in the same table as the formula cell, or they can be in another table on the same or a different sheet. Cell references have different formats, depending on whether they refer to a single cell or a range of cells, whether the cell's table has headers, and so on.

Table 4.4 lists the formats that Numbers uses for cell references.

For named references, Numbers omits the table or sheet name if the referenced cells have unique names in the spreadsheet.

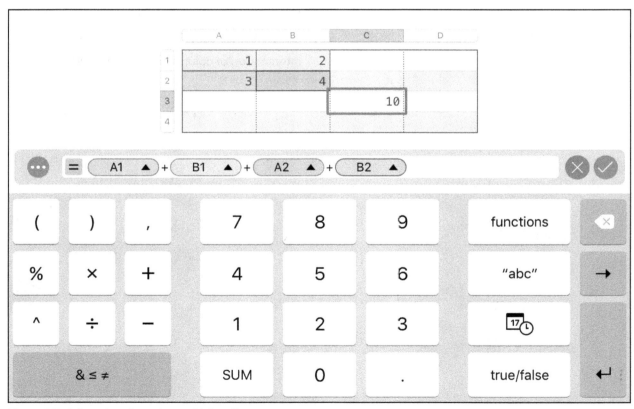

Figure 4.5 A formula referencing multiple cells.

Tip: When referencing a cell in a table that has multiple header rows or columns, Numbers uses the name in the header cell closest to the referenced cell. For example, if a table has two header rows, and A1 contains XXX and A2 contains YYY, when you save a formula that uses a cell in column A, YYY is used in the named reference. (If YYY appears in another header cell in the spreadsheet, however, XXX is used).

Table 4.4 Cell Reference Formats

Reference	Format	Example
A cell in the same table that contains the formula	The cell's reference tab letter (column) followed by its reference tab number (row).	*D3* refers to the third row in the fourth column.
A range of cells	A colon (:) between the first and last cell in the range, using reference tab notation.	*D1:E4* refers to the first four cells in both the fourth and fifth columns (eight cells total).
All cells in a column	The header-column name or the column letter.	*D* refers to all the cells in the fourth column. *Test 2* refers to all the cells in the column whose header is Test 2.
All cells in a range of columns	A colon (:) between the header-column names or the letters of the first and last columns in the range.	*C:D* refers to all the cells in the third and fourth columns. *Test 1:Test 4* refers to all the cells in the columns whose headers range from Test 1 to Test 4, inclusive.
All cells in a row	The header-row name or row-number:row-number.	*2:2* refers to all the cells in the second row. *Div44* refers to all the cells in the row whose header is Div44.
All cells in a range of rows	A colon (:) between the header-row names or the row numbers of the first and last rows in the range.	*1:5* refers to all the cells in the first five rows. *Div11:Div44* refers to all the cells in the rows whose headers range from Div11 to Div44, inclusive.
A cell in a table that has a header column and a header row	The header-column name followed by the header-row name.	*Qtr2 Div44* refers to a cell whose header column is Qtr2 and whose header row is Div44.
A cell in another table on the same sheet	The table name followed by two colons (::) and then the cell reference.	*Table 2::C5* refers to cell C5 in the table named Table 2. *Profits::Qtr2 Div44* refers to a cell by name.
A cell in a table on another sheet	The sheet name followed by two colons (::), the table name, two colons (::), and then the cell reference.	*Sheet 1::Table 2::C5* refers to cell C5 in the table named Table 2 on a sheet named Sheet 1. *Reports::Profits::Qtr2 Div44* refers to a cell by name.

Inserting cell references

When you build a formula, you don't type the cell references yourself—Numbers inserts them for you when you select cells. A reference appears in the formula bar as a colored oval placeholder holding the name or reference-tab address of the cell(s). The color of each placeholder is coordinated to match the highlight color of the corresponding cells in the table. In Figure 4.6, cell D6 references the two cells to its left. Color-matching makes it clear which cells you're using in the formula. Color highlighting appears only when you're editing a formula.

You can redefine any cell reference in your formula. Tap a cell reference in the formula bar to show color-coded circular **selection handles** in the corners of each block of referenced cells. To redefine a reference in the formula, drag the selection handles to expand or shrink the range, or drag the selection box itself to a new location (Figure 4.7).

To insert a cell reference in a formula:

1   In the formula bar, position the insertion point where you want the reference to appear or, to replace an existing reference, tap its placeholder to select it.

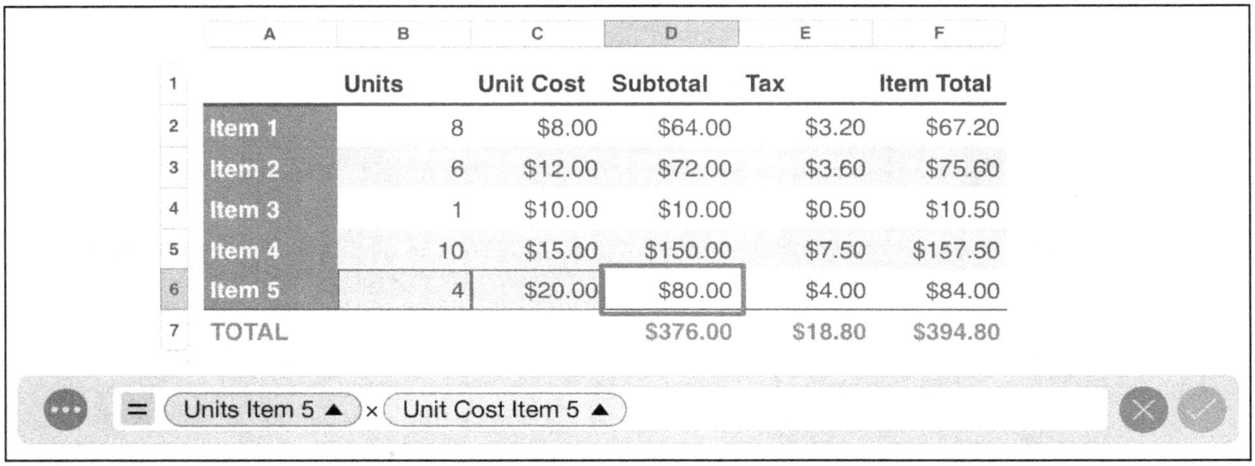

	A	B	C	D	E	F
1		Units	Unit Cost	Subtotal	Tax	Item Total
2	Item 1	8	$8.00	$64.00	$3.20	$67.20
3	Item 2	6	$12.00	$72.00	$3.60	$75.60
4	Item 3	1	$10.00	$10.00	$0.50	$10.50
5	Item 4	10	$15.00	$150.00	$7.50	$157.50
6	Item 5	4	$20.00	$80.00	$4.00	$84.00
7	TOTAL			$376.00	$18.80	$394.80

= (Units Item 5 ▲) × (Unit Cost Item 5 ▲)

Figure 4.6 Color-coded cell references are highlighted in the table and formula bar.

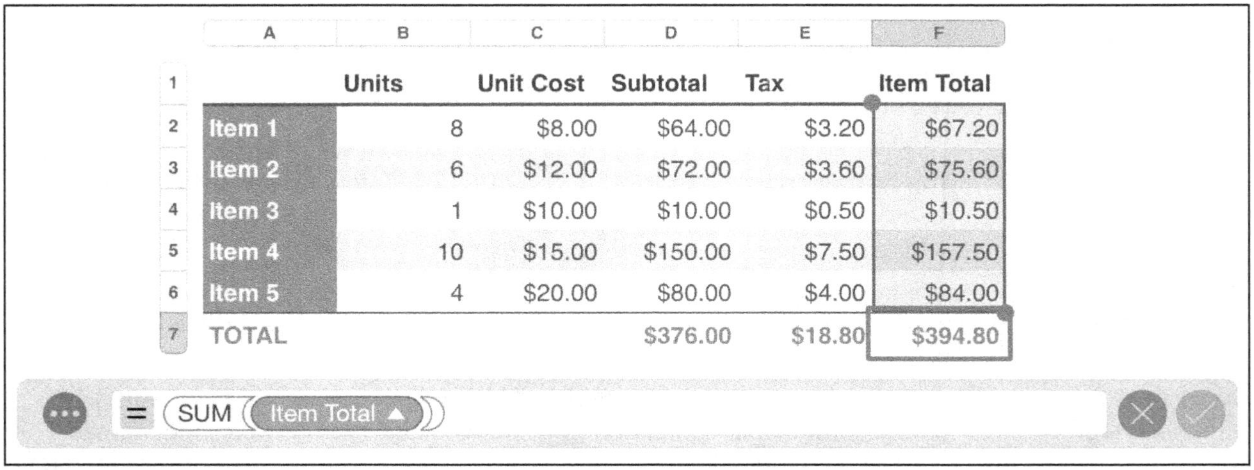

	A	B	C	D	E	F
1		Units	Unit Cost	Subtotal	Tax	Item Total
2	Item 1	8	$8.00	$64.00	$3.20	$67.20
3	Item 2	6	$12.00	$72.00	$3.60	$75.60
4	Item 3	1	$10.00	$10.00	$0.50	$10.50
5	Item 4	10	$15.00	$150.00	$7.50	$157.50
6	Item 5	4	$20.00	$80.00	$4.00	$84.00
7	TOTAL			$376.00	$18.80	$394.80

= (SUM ((Item Total ▲)))

Figure 4.7 You can drag the selection handles or the selection box to redefine a reference in a formula.

2   Do any of the following:

- ▸ To refer to a single cell, tap the cell.

- ▸ To refer to a range of cells, touch and hold a cell in a corner of the range and then drag across the range.

- ▸ To refer to all cells in a column, tap the column's letter on the reference tab. To refer to multiple columns, touch and hold a column letter and then drag left or right.

  In Figure 4.8, the multicolumn reference spans four columns (Test 1:Test 4). Header and footer cells are ignored when you select entire columns or rows, though you can re-define the range to include them.

- ▸ To refer to all cells in a row, tap the row's number on the reference tab. To refer to multiple rows, touch and hold a row number and then drag up or down.

- ▸ To refer to cells in a different table on the same sheet, tap the target table and then select a reference as described above.

- ▸ To refer to cells in a table on a different sheet, tap the sheet tab, tap the table, and then select a reference as described above.

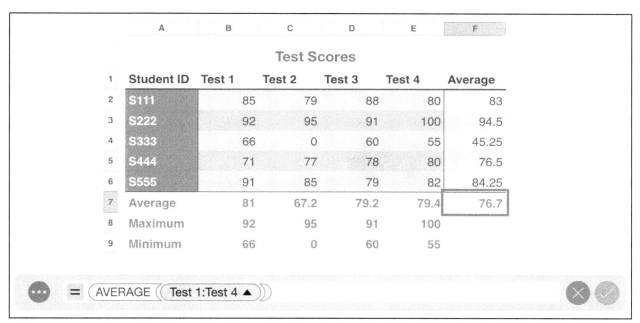

Figure 4.8 A multicolumn reference.

Summing Values Quickly

Numbers offers a few tricks that let you sum values quickly.

- To sum a column of values, double-tap an empty cell at the bottom of the column, bring up the formula keyboard, and then tap the SUM key. Numbers auto-inserts the SUM function with a column reference.

- To sum a group of noncontiguous cells, bring up the formula keyboard and then start tapping cells. Numbers auto-inserts a + operator between each pair of references, creating a sum.

- To sum a block of neighboring cells, summon the formula keyboard and drag over the range of cells. Instead of using the + operator, Numbers uses the SUM function with a reference to your cell selection.

Comparison Operators

You can use comparison operators to base a formula's result on whether a certain condition is satisfied.

Comparison operator basics

The **comparison operators**, listed in Table 4.5, compare two values and evaluate to TRUE or FALSE (that is, to a boolean value). Comparison operators are also called **relational** or **logical operators**.

The data type determines how values are compared:

- Numeric values compare arithmetically. < means *smaller*, and > means *larger*. (To compare floating-point numbers for equality, use the DELTA function.)

- Text strings compare lexicographically. < means *precedes*, and > means *follows*. Text comparisons are case-insensitive. (To do a case-sensitive comparison, use the EXACT function.)

- Dates and times compare chronologically. < means *earlier*, and > means *later*. Dates and times must have the same fields (year, month, day, hour, and so on) to be compared meaningfully.

- Durations compare by length. < means *shorter*, and > means *longer*.

- For boolean values, TRUE > FALSE (and FALSE < TRUE) because TRUE is interpreted as 1 and FALSE is interpreted as 0. (The checkbox cell format (page 44) uses boolean values.)

- You can use a numeric expression in place of a boolean one. If the expression evaluates to 0, Numbers considers it to be FALSE; any other number is considered to be TRUE.

- When you sort rows based on a column that contains boolean values, TRUE is interpreted as 1 and FALSE is interpreted as 0. See "Sorting Rows in a Table" on page 58.

Avoid comparing values of different data types. Numbers typically flags such comparisons as errors (page 82), but there are a few situations where such comparisons are valid:

- Text strings compare greater than numbers. For example, "text" > 5, "5" > 5, and "" > 0 all return TRUE.

- Boolean values compare unequally to numbers. For example, TRUE = 1 and FALSE = 0 both return FALSE. TRUE ≠ 1 returns TRUE.

- Boolean values compare unequally to text strings. TRUE = "text" and FALSE = "FALSE" both return FALSE. TRUE ≠ "TRUE" returns TRUE.

Comparison operators have lower precedence than arithmetic operators (page 62) and functions (page 74). The expression SUM(A2, B2) + 5 > 10, for example, evaluates as ((SUM(A2, B2)) + 5) > 10. See also "Evaluation Order" on page 66.

Table 4.5 Comparison Operators

Operator	Determines Whether	Example	Result
=	Two values are equal	"XYZ" = "xyz"	TRUE
≠	Two values are not equal	2 ≠ 2	FALSE
<	The first value is less than the second value	"ace" < "king"	TRUE
≤	The first value is less than or equal to the second value	1-Dec-2014 ≤ 1-Nov-2015	TRUE
>	The first value is greater than the second value	2 days > 1 week	FALSE
≥	The first value is greater than or equal to the second value	0 ≥ −1	TRUE

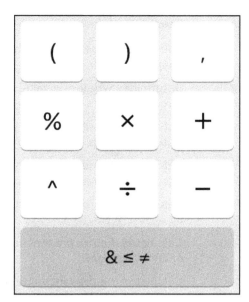

Figure 4.9 The comparison-operator keypad.

The & Operator

The & (ampersand) operator on the comparison-operator keypad joins (concatenates) text strings. If A1 contains "aaa", B1 contains "bbb", and C1 contains "ccc", then the formula

```
=A1 & B1 & C1
```

returns "aaabbbccc".

You must add whitespace or delimiters (field separators) between the strings manually:

```
=A1 & ", " & B1 & ", " & C1
```

returns "aaa, bbb, ccc". The constant text values in the above formula are surrounded by quotation marks.

As an alternative to the & operator, you can use the CONCATENATE function.

Inserting comparison operators

You can use cell references or constants in comparisons. The expression A1=A2, for example, is TRUE if cell A1 contains the same value as cell A2. Comparison operations are used mainly in IF, AND, OR, NOT, SUMIF, COUNTIF, and other functions that take expressions that can be evaluated as TRUE or FALSE. For example, the formula

```
=IF(C2=0,0,C1/C2)
```

uses a comparison to avoid dividing by zero.

Comparisons don't have to be embedded in functions; you can type them as stand-alone formulas. For example, the formula

```
=A1=5
```

will display TRUE or FALSE in a cell depending on the value in A1. Note that it's clearer to enter this formula as

```
=(A1=5)
```

To insert a comparison operator in a formula:

1   In the formula bar, position the insertion point where you want the operator to appear.

2   If the comparison-operator keys aren't visible on the left side of the formula keyboard, tap the &≤≠ key. (Tapping the ()+÷ key switches backs to the arithmetic operators.)

3   Tap an operator key (Figure 4.9).

Functions

Functions are built-in, specialized, named operations that you can use in your formulas. You can combine functions with constants, operators, and cell references to create powerful formulas. Numbers provides more than 250 functions, ranging from simple ones that sum or average numbers to complex ones that do financial and engineering calculations. In addition to working with numbers, functions can do calendar arithmetic, make logical decisions, search and transform text, and look up values in lists.

Numbers has a complete help page for every function. These pages are also published in the *iWork Formulas and Functions User Guide*, available for download in PDF format at *support.apple.com/manuals/iwork*. (Numbers for iOS uses a large subset of Numbers for Mac functions.) Table 4.6 lists some of the most commonly used functions.

Tip: You can't create custom functions in Numbers as you can in Excel—Numbers has no equivalent of Visual Basic for Applications (VBA).

Table 4.6 Commonly Used Functions

Function	Description
AND/OR/NOT	Creates a conditional formula that results in a boolean value
AVERAGE	Calculates the arithmetic mean of a group of numbers
CONVERT	Converts a number from one measurement system to another system
COUNT	Counts the number of numbers or dates in a range
DATEDIF	Calculates the time difference between two dates
FIND/SEARCH	Finds one text string within another
IF	Creates a conditional formula that results in another calculation

Function	Description
INT	Rounds a number down to the nearest integer
ISERROR/IFERROR	Determines whether a value is an error (page 82)
MIN/MAX	Returns the smallest and largest value of a group of numbers
NETWORK-DAYS	Calculates the number of working days between two dates
NOW	Returns the current date and time
NPV	Calculates the net present value of an investment
PV	Calculates the present value of a series of regular periodic cash flows
RAND/RAND-BETWEEN	RAND returns a uniform random number between 0 and 1. RAND-BETWEEN returns a uniform random integer between specified lower and upper bounds; see "Calculating Random Numbers" on page 60
REPLACE/SUBSTITUTE	Replaces one text string with another
ROUND	Rounds a number to the specified number of decimal places
SQRT	Returns the square root of a number
SUM	Calculates the sum of a group of numbers
TODAY	Returns the current date
TRIM	Removes extra spaces from text
UPPER/LOWER/PROPER	Changes the case of text
VALUE	Converts text to a number
VLOOKUP/HLOOKUP/LOOKUP	Looks up values in a list

Function basics

Each function has a name followed by zero or more comma-separated arguments enclosed in parentheses. You use **arguments** to provide the values that the function needs to do its work. The CONVERT function, for example, takes a number in one measurement system and converts it to another system. Its **syntax**—which gives a function's name and the names and order of its arguments—is

CONVERT(*convert-num, from-unit, to-unit*)

Using CONVERT with sample arguments gives the formula

=CONVERT(100,"C","F")

This formula displays 212 in a cell—100 degrees Celsius expressed in the Fahrenheit scale, and

=CONVERT(25,"km","mi")

displays the number of miles in 25 kilometers (15.53427...).

In Figure 4.10, the CONVERT functions in the last column get their arguments from the first three columns by using cell references.

The number and types of arguments vary by function. You can type arguments directly into the formula or use cell references for some or all arguments. Arguments can be constants, operator expressions, cell references, or other functions. Text arguments must go inside quotation marks (but don't put cell references inside quotation marks—they aren't considered to be text even if their cells contain text). Here are a few examples of valid arguments:

=CONVERT(60+40,"C","F")

=CONVERT(A2,B2,C2)

=CONVERT(A2+10,B2,UPPER("f"))

=CONVERT(SUM(D2:D10)+SUM(F2:F10)-273.15,B2,UPPER(LEFT("fahrenheit",1)))

Functions that take no arguments need no user-supplied data to do their work. The TODAY function, for example, returns today's date:

=TODAY()

Functions have higher precedence than arithmetic operators (page 62) and comparison operators (page 72). The expression SUM(A2, B2) + 5 > 10, for example, evaluates as ((SUM(A2, B2)) + 5) > 10. See also "Evaluation Order" on page 66.

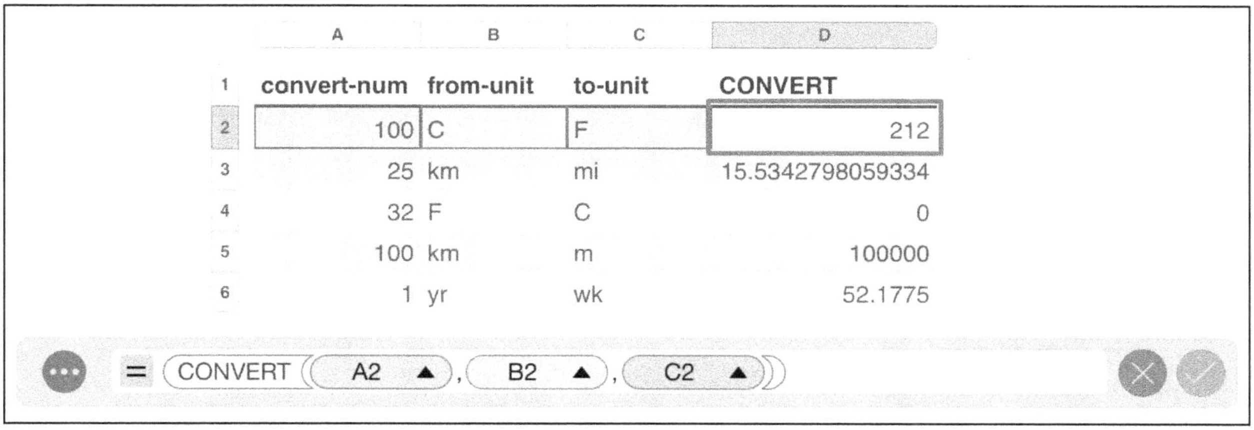

	A	B	C	D
1	convert-num	from-unit	to-unit	CONVERT
2	100	C	F	212
3	25	km	mi	15.5342798059334
4	32	F	C	0
5	100	km	m	100000
6	1	yr	wk	52.1775

= CONVERT(A2 ▲ , B2 ▲ , C2 ▲)

Figure 4.10 Example function arguments.

Inserting functions

A function can be one of several elements in a formula, or it can be the only element in a formula. When you build a formula, you don't type the function names yourself—you use the **function browser** to insert them. The function browser lets you flick through Numbers' entire library of functions. When you find the function you want, Numbers inserts it into your formula, including gray-oval argument placeholders. The placeholder of the selected argument is highlighted in blue (Figure 4.11).

In Figure 4.12, the arguments for the function in cell F2 are all cell references, except for the last argument, which is optional and, here, omitted.

If an argument takes only a limited number of discrete values, its placeholder will show a triangle.

You can tap this triangle for a pop-up menu of choices (Figure 4.13). Tap a menu entry to fill in the argument, or tap off the menu to leave the argument unchanged.

To insert a function in a formula:

1 In the formula bar, position the insertion point where you want the function to appear or, to replace an existing function, tap its name to select it.

2 Tap the functions key on the keyboard and do one of the following:

   ▶ To access all Numbers' functions, tap Categories, tap a category, and then tap a function. (To see every function, tap the All category.)

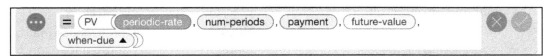

Figure 4.11 Function argument placeholders.

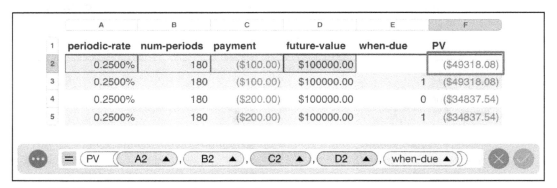

Figure 4.12 Here, function arguments are cell references.

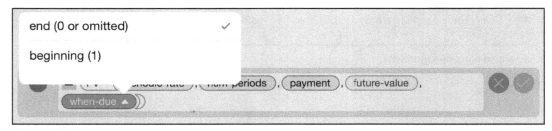

Figure 4.13 For some function arguments, valid argument values are listed in a pop-up menu.

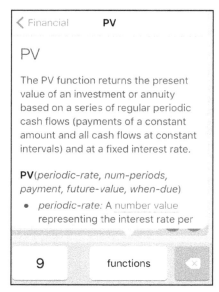

Figure 4.14 Pop-up function help.

Optional Arguments

Some functions take **optional arguments**. If you omit an optional argument from the function, Numbers uses a **default value** when it evaluates the function. If you want to use a value other than the default, specify an optional argument just as you would a required one. The LOG function, for example, returns the logarithm of a positive number by using a specified base. LOG has two arguments:

LOG(*pos-num*, *base*)

The first argument is required; the second is optional. (Optional arguments, if they exist, always follow required ones.) If you omit *base*, it is assumed to be 10. Hence

=LOG(100)

is the same as

=LOG(100,10)

A function's help window tells you whether an argument is required or optional and, for the latter, gives its default value. If you omit some optional arguments but not others, don't delete the commas between them.

▶ To access a function that you've used recently, tap Recent and then tap a function. Each time you use a function, Numbers inserts it at the top of the Recent list and removes the least recently used (bottommost) function.

▶ To get help with a function, tap ⓘ next to its name (Figure 4.14). After you finish reading, tap ‹ at the top of the window to return to the list of functions, and then tap a function. The help window includes a function's name, purpose, and syntax, as well as descriptions of arguments, usage notes, examples, and links to related functions. (To open the help window of a function within the formula bar, tap the function name to select it, and then tap the name again.)

Numbers inserts the function and its argument placeholder(s) in the formula bar.

3 In the formula bar, tap each argument placeholder and do one of the following:

▶ To insert a cell reference, tap a cell or drag across a cell range.

▶ To insert a nested function, tap the functions key.

▶ To insert an arithmetic operator or a comparison operator, tap an operator key on the formula keyboard. To switch between the operators, tap the &≤≠ or ()+÷ key.

▶ To insert a number, tap the number keys on the formula keyboard.

▶ To insert text, tap the "abc" key.

▶ To insert a date, time, or duration, tap the 🗓 key.

▶ To insert a boolean value, tap the true/false key.

▶ To omit an optional argument, leave its placeholder as is. Or, to delete the placeholder, tap the placeholder to select it, tap it again, and then tap Cut in the pop-up menu.

Copying and Moving Formulas

When you copy or move cells containing numbers, text, or other raw values, Numbers duplicates the value in the target cells. Copying and moving formulas, however, is complicated by cell references (page 67), which you may not want to duplicate. Numbers' default behavior is what you want most of the time:

- When you *move* a formula cell, Numbers leaves its original cell references untouched; in its new location, the formula still points to the same cells that it used to.

- When you *copy* a formula cell, Numbers updates the formula's cell references so that they point to different cells relative to the formula's new location.

In Figure 4.15, the original formula, in cell C1, sums cells A1 and B1.

When you *move* C1 to C2, the cell references don't change: the formula still sums A1 and B1 (Figure 4.16).

When you *copy* C1 to C2 and C3, the cell references change: each copied formula sums the two cells to its left—the same relative position of the referenced cells in the original formula (Figure 4.17).

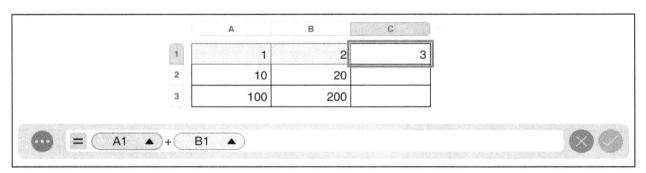

Figure 4.15 The original formula.

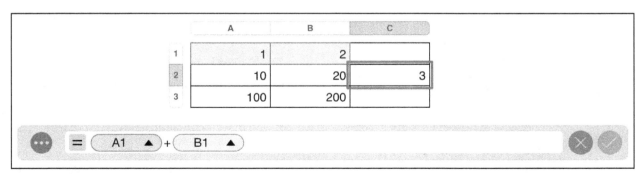

Figure 4.16 The moved formula.

You can move formulas by dragging. You can copy formulas by cut-and-paste, copy-and-paste, or filling. These techniques are covered in "Cutting, Copying, and Pasting Cells" on page 50 and "Filling Cells with Data Series" on page 54. You might think that cut-and-paste moves a cell, but it actually copies it—it only looks moved because its contents disappear from its original location. Numbers considers all pasted cells to be copies of the original.

When you paste a formula, tap Paste Formulas in the pop-up menu (Figure 4.18). Tapping Paste Values pastes the result of the formula but not the actual formula—which is handy when you have a result that you no longer want to update.

To copy the *text* of a formula, double-tap an empty area of the formula bar and tap Select All in the pop-up menu. (To copy only part of the text, drag the blue selection handles ● to encompass the characters that you want to copy.) Tap Copy in the pop-up menu. When you paste the formula's text in a new cell, all the cell references stay the same as they were in the original.

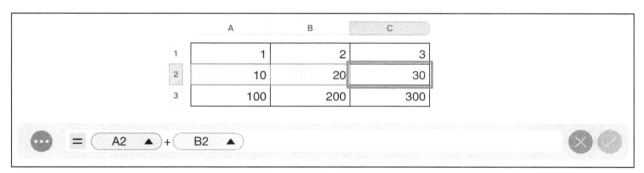

Figure 4.17 The copied formula.

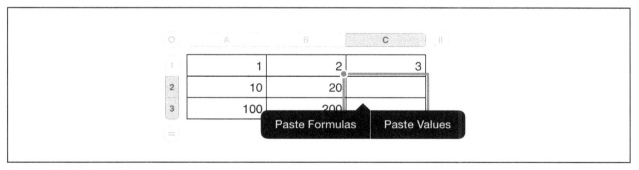

Figure 4.18 The Paste Formulas/Values menu.

Relative vs. absolute cell references

By default, cell addresses in formulas are **relative cell references**, meaning their row or column addresses can change when you copy formulas. For situations where you want to preserve row or column positions, Numbers offers **absolute cell references**, which freeze cell addresses no matter where you copy formula cells.

To set relative and absolute cell references:

1   In the formula bar, tap the triangle in the placeholder of the cell reference that you want to preserve.

2   Change Preserve Row or Preserve Column to On (absolute) or Off (relative) for the beginning or end addresses of the selected range. A $ character in the cell reference indicates an absolute row or column:

   Relative column–relative row (A1). When the formula cell is copied, the cell reference changes so that it retains the same position relative to the formula cell.

   Absolute column–absolute row (A1). When the formula cell is copied, the cell reference doesn't change.

   Relative column–absolute row (A$1). When the formula cell is copied, only the column component can change to retain its position relative to the formula cell.

   Absolute column–relative row ($A1). When the formula cell is copied, only the row component can change to retain its position relative to the formula cell.

In Figure 4.19, the formula in cell C1 sums cells A1 and B1, but uses the absolute cell reference A1. The B1 reference is relative.

When copying the formula, the B1 reference changes to B2, but A1 stays anchored (Figure 4.20).

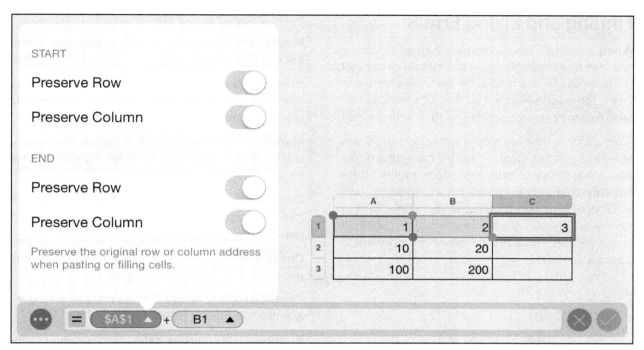

Figure 4.19 A cell with mixed relative and absolute references.

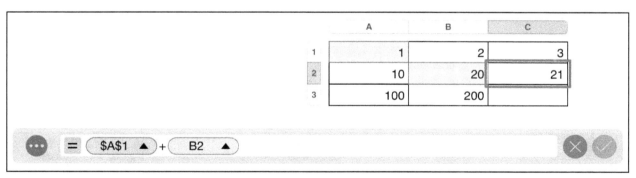

Figure 4.20 The copied cell retains its absolute reference but not its relative reference.

Finding and Fixing Errors

When a formula cell contains an error, Numbers displays a red triangle 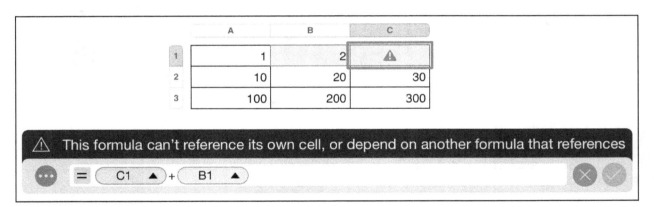 in the middle of the cell. Double-tap the cell to see the error message and fix the formula. In Figure 4.21, Cell C1's formula contains a circular reference: it refers to directly to itself.

Formulas that reference cells with errors are themselves flagged as errors, possibly causing a ripple effect that fills your table with red triangles. Unfortunately, Numbers for iOS lacks the auditing tools of Excel or Numbers for Mac, so you'll have to hunt for the initial bad cells in the chain. The ISERROR and IFERROR functions are useful for preventing cascading errors.

Some common errors are:

Invalid cell references. Typing or pasting a reference to nonexistent cell or range name.

Syntax errors. Unpaired parentheses, misplaced operators (2××2), or too many/few function arguments (count the commas).

Math errors. Dividing by zero, taking the square root of a negative number, or taking the log of a nonpositive number.

Domain errors. Comparing values with incompatible data types (2<FALSE) or doing arithmetic on non-numbers (2+"text").

Circular references. Creating a formula that depends, indirectly or directly, on its own value.

Overflows. Calculating numbers that are too big for Numbers to handle (9999^9999).

Problems with merged cells. See "Merging Cells" on page 52.

![An error flagged in a formula showing a spreadsheet table]

	A	B	C
1	1	2	⚠
2	10	20	30
3	100	200	300

⚠ This formula can't reference its own cell, or depend on another formula that references

= (C1 ▲) + (B1 ▲)

Figure 4.21 An error flagged in a formula.

CHAPTER 5

Charts

Trends and comparisons are hard to discern from raw data, so Numbers provides charts to reveal relationships that aren't apparent by staring at rows and columns of numbers. You can choose from many types of charts—bar charts, pie charts, scatter charts, and more—and you have many ways to customize and embellish them. Knowing which chart type to pick isn't always easy, and decorating charts with unnecessary text, lines, shading, and effects will obscure your message.

Chart Essentials

When you add a chart to your spreadsheet, Numbers puts a **placeholder chart** on the current sheet, showing sample (fake) data. Numbers for iOS uses the same chart terms as Excel and Numbers for Mac (Figure 5.1).

Source table. A source table contains the data to graph (Figure 5.2). The chart shows whatever data are selected in the source table; you can select all the table's cells or only some of them. A chart is linked dynamically to its source table—when you change a cell's value or select a different range of cells, the associated chart updates automatically. A table can feed data to multiple charts, and a chart can get data from more than one table.

Data points and data series. The source table for the sample column chart has eight data points (values)—four for each region. Region 1 and Region 2 are called the data series because each region's data points appear as a series of columns of the same color, one column for each year. Each Region 1 column is paired beside its corresponding Region 2 column, and each side-by-side set of columns is called a **data set** or **category** (2014 is a category, 2015 is a category, and so on).

Numbers lets you **transpose** data series to change the emphasis of your data. In Figure 5.3, data points are grouped by region rather than by year. The chart contains two sets of four columns (eight data points). The data points for each year are data series (each series has only two data points) and each region is a category.

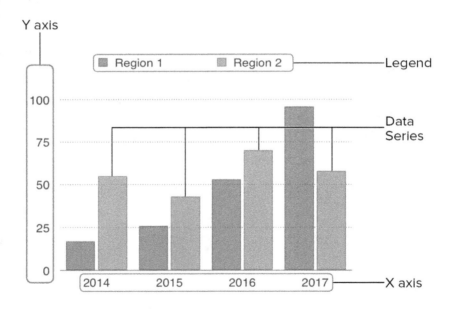

Figure 5.1 A sample chart.

	2014	2015	2016	2017
Region 1	17	26	53	96
Region 2	55	43	70	58

Figure 5.2 The source table for the sample chart.

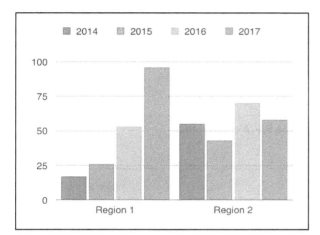

Figure 5.3 The sample chart, transposed.

Legend. The legend shows the colors, symbols, and labels used for each data series in the chart. The legend's labels come from the header rows or columns (page 30) in the source table. You can show or hide the legend.

X axis and y axis. The x axis and the y axis are the horizontal and vertical lines that give a chart scale and context. In column, bar, area, and line charts, data points are plotted on one axis (the y axis for column, area, and line charts; the x axis for bar charts) and categories are grouped on the other axis. The data-point (numeric) axis is called the **value axis**, and the data-set (group) axis is called the **category axis**. In scatter charts, both the x and y axes are value axes. Pie charts have no axes. Category axes are labeled with text from row or column headers in the source table; value axes are labeled with a numeric range. Axes are marked by stepped graduations called **tick marks** and **gridlines**, which you can show, hide, reformat, and (on value axes) rescale.

Picking a Chart Type

Numbers offers different chart types, each of which is designed for certain situations or data types (Figure 5.4). Each chart type has its strengths and weaknesses for different types of data.

Column. Column charts display vertical columns with lengths proportional to the values that they represent (Figure 5.5). They're often used to compare groups over time or rank discrete things by some numeric measure (country on the x axis and population on the y axis, for example). For time series, a line chart can be a better choice.

Stacked Column. Stacked column charts display the results of multiple data series, combined and stacked atop one another like towers of blocks (Figure 5.6). These charts use the same data as regular column charts but emphasize overall effects rather than individual values. It's usually a bad idea to try to estimate or compare the individual values (different colors) within the columns of this type of chart.

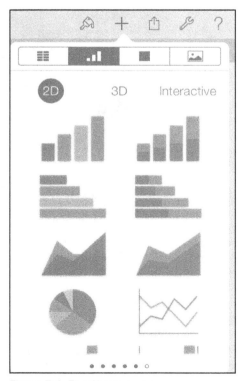

Figure 5.4 The Charts menu.

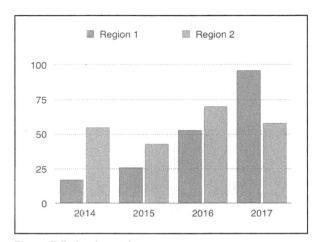

Figure 5.5 A column chart.

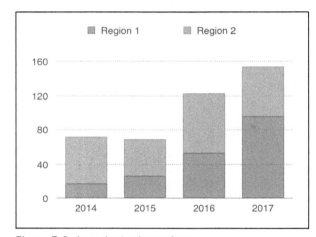

Figure 5.6 A stacked column chart.

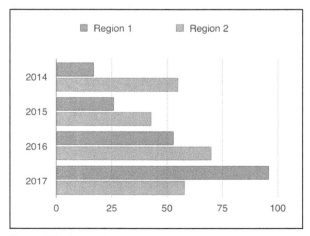

Figure 5.7 A bar chart.

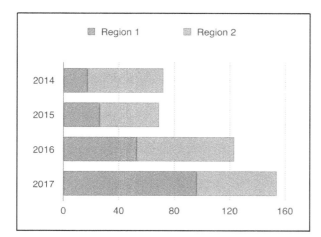

Figure 5.8 A stacked bar chart.

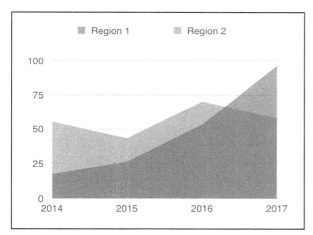

Figure 5.9 An area chart.

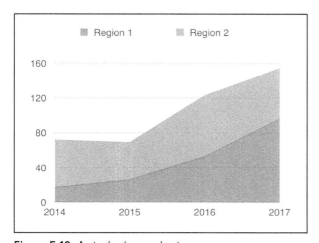

Figure 5.10 A stacked area chart.

Bar. Bar charts are column charts turned sideways; that is, with their axes swapped (Figure 5.7). They're often used to compare the speed or duration of events. Bar charts look best when you hide the x axis and display the values at the end of each bar.

Stacked Bar. Stacked bar charts are like stacked column charts, only sideways, and with the same caveats (Figure 5.8).

Area. Area charts are like line charts but fill in the space below each line (data series) with a different color (Figure 5.9). Like line charts, they're often used to show trends over time. The chief danger of area charts is that data series can cross and obscure each other.

Stacked Area. Like stacked column and bar charts, stacked area charts emphasize overall effects rather than individual values (Figure 5.10). The continuous color and joined line segments "flow" rightward across the chart, so they're better than stacked column charts for comparing groups over time. Unlike regular area charts, stacked area charts pose no danger of obscured data points.

Line. Line charts display data series as points connected by straight line segments (Figure 5.11). They're often used to show trends over time. If you've got a lot of points to plot, line charts are a cleaner and more compact alternative to column charts. A line chart overloaded with five or more lines (data series) is a "spaghetti" chart.

Pie. A pie chart is a circle divided into slices, with each slice showing a percentage of the whole (Figure 5.12). (Technically, the arc length of each sector of the circle—and consequently its area—is proportional to the value it represents.) Pies show proportions, not specific data values, so they work best for graphing a single row or column with few cells. Despite their popularity, pie charts are usually a bad choice. It's hard to compare different slices of a pie, particularly those with similar values (and forget about comparing data across different pies). They're not bad if you want to compare the size of a single slice to the whole pie, but you're almost always better off with a single-series column chart, or even a non-graphical table of values. You can drag slices out of the pie to emphasize them.

Scatter. A scatter chart (also called a scatterplot) displays data differently from the other types of charts: it plots every data point on its own x and y coordinates (Figure 5.13). A scatter chart has two value axes and needs at least two columns or rows of continuous numeric data to plot values for a single data series. To show multiple data series, you use additional two-column (or two-row) pairs. Each pair of data values determines the position of one data point: the first value determines the point's position on the x axis, and the second determines its position on the y axis. Because scatter charts have no category axis, don't convert other types of charts (which don't use paired, or bivariate, data) to scatter charts, or vice versa.

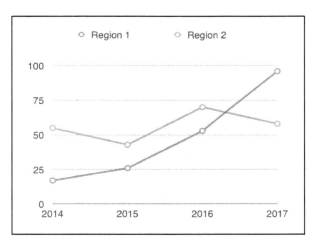

Figure 5.11 A line chart.

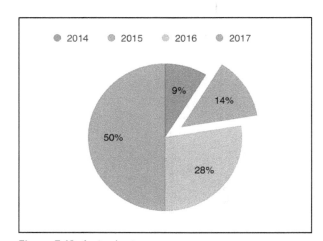

Figure 5.12 A pie chart.

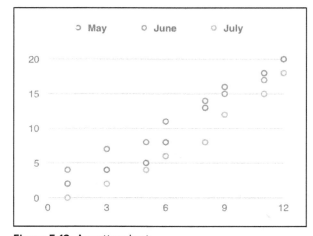

Figure 5.13 A scatter chart.

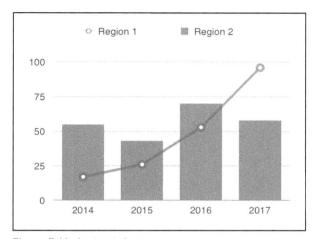

Figure 5.14 A mixed chart.

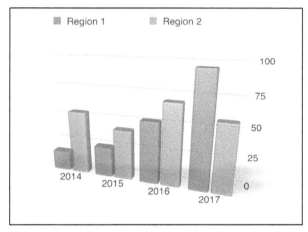

Figure 5.15 A 3D chart.

Mixed. A mixed chart (also called a combination chart) uses two chart types (line and column) to emphasize that the chart contains different kinds of information (Figure 5.14). When the range of values for different data series in your chart varies widely, or when you have mixed types of data, you can plot one or more data series from a different chart type on a secondary y axis.

3D charts. Three-dimensional versions of most of the 2D chart types are available (Figure 5.15). 3D charts obscure and distort data and are generally regarded as useless and amateurish—stick with 2D charts.

Interactive charts. An interactive chart presents data in stages, showing the relationship between different groups of data (Figure 5.16). Drag the slider (or tap the slider's arrows) below an interactive chart to animate how values change over time, by category, by country, or however you've grouped your data series. The name of the group that you're currently viewing appears below the x axis. Interactive charts include column, bar, scatter, and bubble charts.

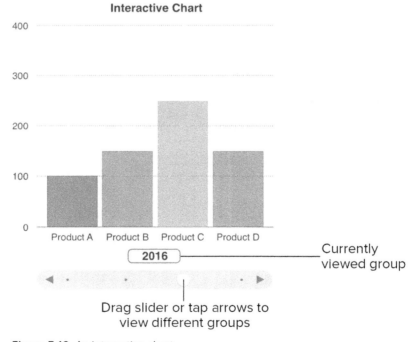

Figure 5.16 An interactive chart.

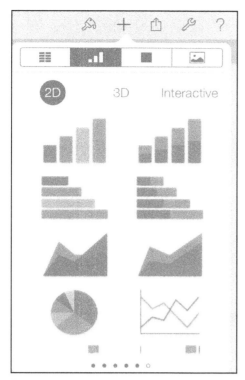

Figure 5.17 The Charts menu.

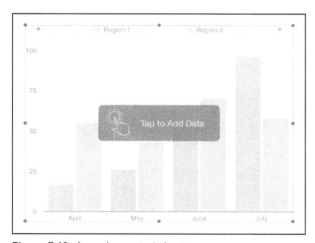

Figure 5.18 A newly created chart.

Creating a Chart

A chart can show all the data in a table or data only in selected cells of one or more tables. You can add, delete, and edit a chart's data series at any time. If a table has header rows or columns (page 30), Numbers uses the header text as axis and legend labels.

To add a blank chart to a sheet:

1   Tap ✛ in the toolbar and then tap ▮▮▮ (Figure 5.17).

    You can choose from a range of preset 2D, 3D, and Interactive chart styles in different colors that match the template you're working in.

2   Tap the chart style that's closest to what you want to use. To see all the chart styles, flick right or left in the Charts menu. (You can also touch and hold a chart, and then drag to position it on the sheet.)

    A placeholder chart appears on the current sheet (Figure 5.18). Whatever the look of the chart you begin with, you can customize it.

3   Do any of the following:

    ▸ To move the chart, drag it.

    ▸ To resize the chart, drag one of the blue selection handles ● on the chart's perimeter (if the handles aren't visible, tap the chart).

    ▸ To layer the chart above or below other objects on the sheet, tap ⌂ in the toolbar, tap Arrange, and then drag the Back/Front slider.

To link a chart to a source table:

1   Tap the chart. You may have to tap twice to show the "Add Data" message box (Figure 5.19).

2   Touch and hold the source table, and then tap and drag to select one or more data series.

   The chart updates instantly as you change the selection. You can select multiple ranges within a table or across multiple tables.

3   Tap Done in the toolbar.

To quickly create a chart from a selected range:

▪   Select the range of cells that you want to chart and then tap Create Chart in the pop-up menu (Figure 5.20).

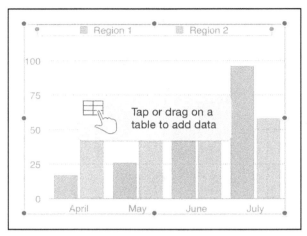

Figure 5.19 A chart ready to be linked.

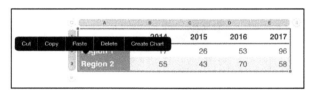

Figure 5.20 Tap Create Chart in the pop-up menu.

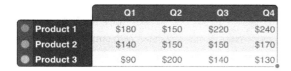

	Q1	Q2	Q3	Q4
Product 1	$180	$150	$220	$240
Product 2	$140	$150	$150	$170
Product 3	$90	$200	$140	$130

	Q1	Q2	Q3	Q4
Product 1	$180	$150	$220	$240
Product 2	$140	$150	$150	$170
Product 3	$90	$200	$140	$130

	Q1	Q2	Q3	Q4
Product 1	$180	$150	$220	$240
Product 2	$140	$150	$150	$170
Product 3	$90	$200	$140	$130

	Q1	Q2	Q3	Q4
Product 1	$180	$150	$220	$240
Product 2	$140	$150	$150	$170
Product 3	$90	$200	$140	$130

Figure 5.21 Example row and column series.

Figure 5.21 shows examples of selected contiguous and noncontiguous row and column series. The easiest way to select a data series is to tap its header row or column, but you can select any range by touching and holding a cell and dragging. If you end up with a mess of ranges and selection handles ●, you can backtrack by deleting one series at a time, or bail out completely by tapping Done and then Undo. (Deleting a source table severs any links that it has to charts, which then revert to placeholder charts.)

To edit data series:

1   Tap the chart, and then tap Edit References in the pop-up menu.

A small triangle appears on the corner tab of each sheet that holds a source table linked to the chart (Figure 5.22).

2   In the linked source table, do any of the following:

▶   To delete a series, tap the dark handle adjacent to the series, and then tap Delete Series (Figure 5.23).

▶   To add a series, touch and hold a cell and drag across a range, or tap a header cell to add an entire row or column.

▶   To swap (transpose) rows and columns as series, tap ⚙ in the toolbar, and then tap your preference (Figure 5.24).

The Plot commands work best if your data series span entire rows or columns.

▶   To resize series individually, tap ⚙ in the toolbar, turn on Show Each Series, and then drag the selection handles ● to encompass the desired range (Figure 5.25).

When Show Each Series is turned off, Numbers shows contiguous data series with a single selection handle, so they can be resized as a group. Turning on Show Each Series gives each series its own selection handle, for individual control.

3   Tap Done in the toolbar.

Tip: You can chart numeric, date, time, and duration values.

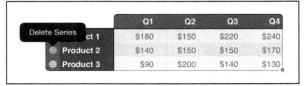

Figure 5.22 A sheet tab with source table triangle.

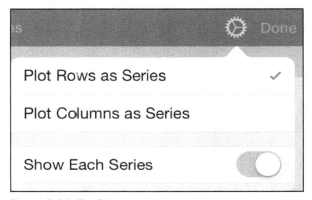

Figure 5.23 You can delete individual data series from a chart.

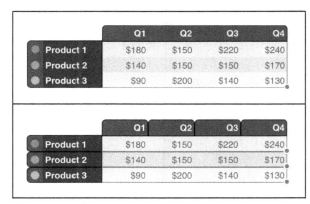

Figure 5.24 The Plot commands transpose rows and columns.

Figure 5.25 The source table when Show Each Series is turned off (top) and turned on (bottom).

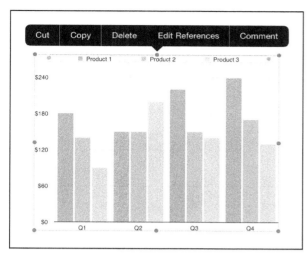

Figure 5.26 The pop-up menu for a chart.

To cut, copy, or delete a chart:

1   Tap the chart to select it, and then tap Cut, Copy, or Delete in the pop-up menu (Figure 5.26).

Cut removes the chart so that it can be moved (pasted) elsewhere. Copy copies a chart so that it can be duplicated (pasted) elsewhere, leaving the original chart intact. Delete removes the chart (without placing a copy on the clipboard).

2   To paste a cut or copied chart, go to the destination (which can be on the same sheet, on a different sheet, or on a sheet in a different spreadsheet), tap an empty area on the sheet, and then tap Paste in the pop-up menu.

Pasted charts within the same spreadsheet still reference their original source tables. If you paste a chart into a different spreadsheet file, Numbers severs the chart's links to the original source table and pastes a new source table along with the chart. This table contains a copy of all the chart's original data series. If the chart referenced multiple source tables, all the original tables' data series are consolidated in the new table. You can also paste charts from Numbers into Keynote and Pages documents (the source data is copied along with the chart).

Formatting a Chart

You can change a chart's type, color scheme, fonts, text size, title, labels, gridlines, tick marks, and more. Experiment to learn the effects of the options: change them and watch how the chart updates.

To format a chart:

1   Tap the chart to select it.

2   Tap 🔨 in the toolbar. You may have to flick up and down in the 🔨 menu to see all the chart options.

3   To change the chart's color scheme, tap Chart and then tap the look you want (Figure 5.27). The colors are preset to match the template you're using.

4   To change the chart type, tap Chart > Chart Options > Chart Type (Figure 5.28). See "Picking a Chart Type" on page 86.

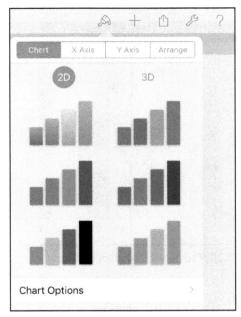

Figure 5.27 The Chart menu.

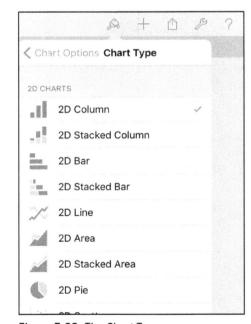

Figure 5.28 The Chart Type menu.

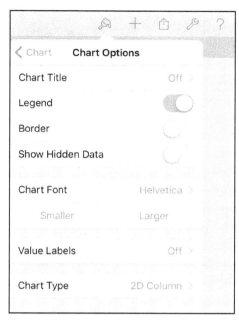

Figure 5.29 The Chart Options menu.

Figure 5.30 The Y Axis menu.

5 To change the font and text size, and to show or hide the title, legend, border, hidden cells, value labels, and more, tap Chart > Chart Options (Figure 5.29).

6 To show, hide, or edit axis lines, reference lines, labels, and markings, tap X Axis or Y Axis (Figure 5.30).

The options for a value (Y) axis let you rescale the chart manually. Tap Value Scale Settings to set the minimum and maximum values of the axis. If your data values are all positive and spread over a very large range (orders of magnitude), try turning on the Log (logarithmic transformation) option to tighten the range and induce symmetry.

Tip: To orient a 3D chart, tap the chart and then drag the rotation control ⊕ that overlays the chart (Figure 5.31).

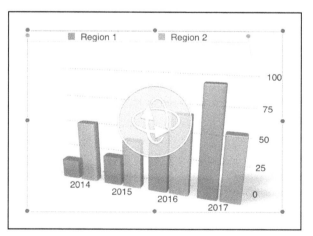

Figure 5.31 A 3D chart with rotation control.

To edit a chart title or axis title:

1 Tap the chart to select it.

2 Double-tap the title and then enter a new title by using the standard text selection and editing commands (Figure 5.32). For editing tips, see "Editing Cells" on page 34. You may need to zoom in on the chart to select or double-tap a title accurately.

To move or resize the legend:

1 Tap the chart to select it.

2 If the chart's title is turned on and overlaps the legend, you may have to turn off the title temporarily to select the legend: tap 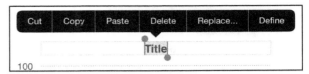, tap Chart, tap Chart Options, and then turn off Chart Title.

3 Touch and hold the center of the legend, and then drag to position it. You can drag it beyond the chart's current bounding box.

4 To resize the legend, drag one of its green selection handles ● (Figure 5.33).

5 If necessary, turn the chart's title back on.

Figure 5.32 Editing a chart title.

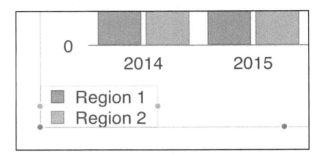

Figure 5.33 You can move and resize a chart legend.

CHAPTER 6

Media, Text Boxes, and Shapes

You can embellish your spreadsheets with various objects and media:

- Text boxes
- Lines
- Arrows
- Geometric shapes
- Photos and other images
- Videos

Creating Objects

An **object** is any item that you add to a sheet and can manipulate. Images, videos, and text boxes are objects, as are lines, arrows, shapes, tables, and charts.

All objects other than images and videos are built in to Numbers. You can use photos or videos taken with iPad 2 or later, or import photos or videos directly from a digital camera, iPhone, iPod touch, or SD memory card by using the Lightning to SD Card Camera Reader, Lightning to USB Camera Adapter, or (for the iPad 3 or earlier) Apple iPad Camera Connection Kit. To sync photos with your computer, use iTunes. The iPad and Numbers support standard photo formats: JPEG, TIFF, GIF, and PNG. You can export videos from video-editing software (such as iMovie or Windows Movie Maker) to iTunes in M4V, MP4, or MOV format. Once in iTunes, videos can be synced to your iPad. Synchronizing with iTunes is covered in the *iPad User Guide* at *help. apple.com/ipad*.

To add a text box, line, arrow, or shape:

1   Tap ➕ in the toolbar and then tap ▉ (Figure 6.1).

    The colors and styles of the objects are preset to match the template you're using. Flick left or right to see all the options.

2   To add an object, tap its icon. Alternatively, touch and hold an icon and then drag it to the sheet.

3   To reposition the object, drag it.

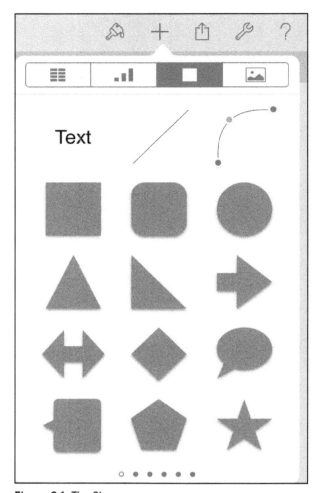

Figure 6.1 The Shapes menu.

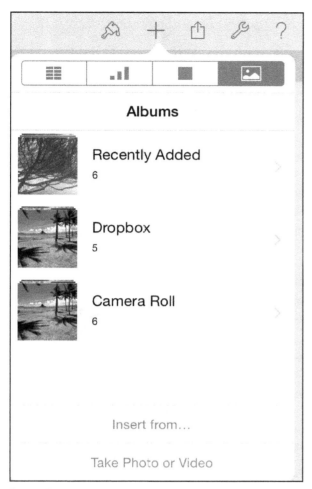

Figure 6.2 The Media menu.

To add an image or video:

1 Tap ✛ in the toolbar and then tap ⊡ (Figure 6.2).

2 To add an image or video, tap its icon. Alternatively, touch and hold an icon and then drag it to the sheet. You can also take photos and videos without leaving the app.

3 To reposition the image or video, drag it.

Working with Images

After adding an image, you can mask it to hide or zoom parts of it. For other tasks, see "Styling Objects" on page 108 and "Arranging Objects" on page 110.

Some of the images that come with the built-in templates are **placeholder images**, which sport a badge ⊕ for quick access to the photos window.

An image's **mask** determines which part of the picture is visible. Changing the mask doesn't edit or permanently crop the image.

To replace a placeholder image:

1 Tap ⊕ at the bottom of the image placeholder (Figure 6.3).

   In the photos window, tap or shoot the replacement image. The image appears within a rectangular mask, so it may be cropped (to fix it, see below).

2 Tap anywhere outside the image.

To mask an image:

1 Double-tap the image.

   The image mask appears (Figure 6.4).

2 Do any of the following:

   ▶ To resize the image within the mask, drag the slider below the image.

   ▶ To resize the mask, drag the blue selection handles ● on the mask's perimeter.

   ▶ To change the part of the image that's visible within the mask, drag the image.

   ▶ To restore the original mask, tap 🖼, tap Image, and then tap Reset Mask.

3 When you're finished, tap Done or tap anywhere outside the image.

Figure 6.3 Tap + to replace a placeholder image.

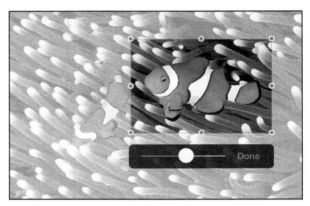

Figure 6.4 An image mask.

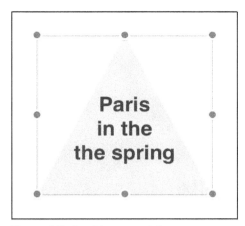

Figure 6.5 An object containing text.

Figure 6.6 An object containing overset text.

Working with Text

After adding a text box or shape, you can double-tap it to add text by using the standard text selection and editing commands (see "Editing Cells" on page 34). You can format selected text by applying preset paragraph styles or by customizing the font, typeface, size, color, alignment, and other attributes (Figure 6.5).

If an object is too small to display all the text that it contains, a ⊞ appears on the object's border (Figure 6.6). **Overset text** in an object isn't visible. Possible fixes: increase the size of the object, decrease the font size, delete some text, or increase the number of columns.

Applying paragraph and character styles

Paragraph styles (Title, Subtitle, Body, and so on) apply to entire paragraphs. Even if you select only a portion of text within a paragraph, the whole paragraph is restyled. If you're applying a style to only one paragraph, just tap so the blinking insertion point appears anywhere in the paragraph, and then tap a style. You can't rename or edit the built-in paragraph styles or create new ones. **Character styles** (bold, italic, underline, and strikethrough) override paragraph styles and apply only to the selected text (to select text, see "Selecting and editing text" on page 36).

To apply a paragraph style:

1 Double-tap the text box or shape containing the text to format.

2 Tap anywhere in the paragraph whose style you want to change, or select multiple paragraphs.

3 Tap in the toolbar, and then tap Style (Figure 6.7). The paragraph styles are preset to match the template you're using. Flick up or down to see them all.

To apply a character style:

1 Double-tap the text box or shape, and then select the target text. (To select a word, double-tap it. To select a paragraph, triple-tap it.)

2 Tap in the toolbar, and then tap Style (Figure 6.8). You can turn the style buttons on and off independently to apply any combination of bold, italic, underline, and strikethrough (Figure 6.9).

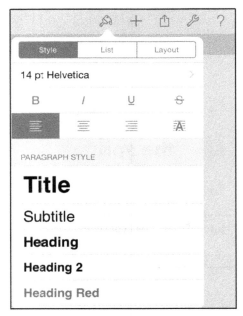

Figure 6.7 The Style menu (paragraph styles).

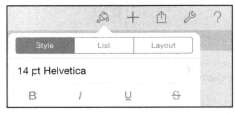

Figure 6.8 The Style menu (character styles).

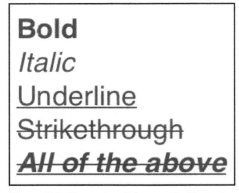

Figure 6.9 Character styles applied to text.

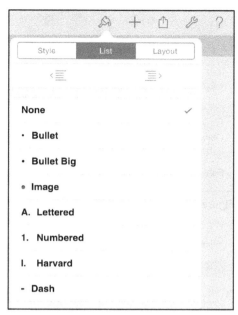

Figure 6.10 The List menu.

- Bulleted list
- Bulleted list
    1. Numbered sublist
    2. Numbered sublist
        A. Lettered sub-sublist
        B. Lettered sub-sublist
- Bulleted list

Figure 6.11 Paragraphs in list format.

Creating lists

You can format any series of paragraphs as a bulleted, lettered, or numbered list. List items can be reordered or indented to create sublists.

To create a list by applying styles:

1 Double-tap the text box or shape and then select the target paragraph(s).

2 Tap ⚒, tap List, and then tap the list type (Figure 6.10). Numbers and letters auto-increment for each new paragraph.

3 Tap the arrows at the top of the menu to indent or un-indent list items. Using different list styles for each indent level shows the hierarchy of information clearly (Figure 6.11).

To create a list by typing:

1 Double-tap the text box or shape containing the text to format.

2 Tap to place the insertion point where you want to start the list.

3 Type the character 1, A, a, I, or i, followed by a dot, followed by a space. Or type a - (hyphen) followed by a space.

4 Type the first list item, and then tap Return.

5 Continue typing list items, tapping Return to add each new item.

6 When you're finished, double-tap Return to end the list.

To reposition an item in a list by dragging:

1 Touch and hold the list item's bullet icon.

2 Drag the item up or down in the list, or drag it left or right to change its indentation level.

A blue triangle ▼ appears to show the item's new position when you lift your finger.

Changing the text size, color, and font

You can override the paragraph style of any block of text and change its size, color, and font. You can also copy and paste text styles, which is a faster alternative to repeatedly slogging through style menus.

To change the font size, text color, or font:

1 Double-tap the text box or shape, and then select the target text.

2 Tap 🖌, tap Style, and then tap the button showing the name of the current font ("14 pt Helvetica", for example) (Figure 6.12 and Figure 6.13).

3 Do any of the following:

  ▶ To set the font size, tap the up or down Size arrows.

  ▶ To set the text color, tap the Color swatch, flick left or right to see all the template colors, and then tap the color you want. To return to the other options, tap ‹.

  ▶ To set the font, tap Font, flick up or down to see all the fonts, and then tap the font you want. To choose a typeface variation, tap ⓘ next to the font name. To return to the other options, tap ‹.

To copy and paste a text style:

1 Double-tap the text box or shape containing the text whose style you want to copy.

2 Select the text, tap Style in the pop-up menu, and then tap Copy Style.

3 Select another range of text within the spreadsheet.

4 Tap Style in the pop-up menu, and then tap Paste Style. (Pasting styles is a faster alternative to repeatedly slogging through style menus.)

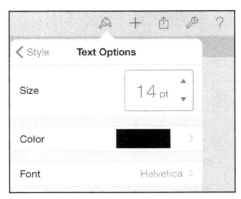

Figure 6.12 The Text Options menu.

Figure 6.13 An example of formatted text.

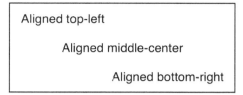

Figure 6.14 An example of text with multiple alignments.

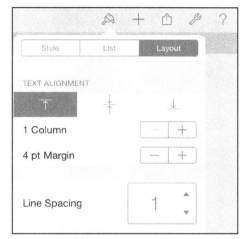

Figure 6.15 The Layout menu.

Figure 6.16 The Style menu.

Changing the text layout

You can change the layout of text within a text box or shape (Figure 6.14).

To change the vertical alignment, number of columns, inset margin, and line spacing:

1 Double-tap the text box or shape, and then select the target text.

2 Tap ✎, and then tap Layout (Figure 6.15).

3 Do any of the following:

▶ Tap the alignment buttons to align text vertically: top, middle, or bottom. (This setting applies to selected paragraphs only.)

▶ Tap the Column – and + buttons to set the number of columns into which the text flows. (This setting applies to all the object's text.)

▶ Tap the Margin – and + buttons to set the distance between the text and the edge of the object's border, measured in points. (This setting applies to all the object's text.)

▶ Tap the Line Spacing up and down arrows to set the amount of whitespace between lines. (This setting applies to selected paragraphs only.)

To change the horizontal alignment:

1 Double-tap the text box or shape, and then select the target text.

2 Tap ✎, and then tap Style (Figure 6.16).

3 Tap the alignment buttons (above "Paragraph Style") to align text horizontally: left, center, right, or justified. (This setting applies to selected paragraphs only.)

To apply objectwide settings quickly:

1 Tap a text box or shape to select it.

2 Tap ✎.

Styling Objects

You can change an object's color, border, shadow, and other style attributes. An object's appearance updates as soon as you change a style option.

If you select multiple objects of the same type (all text boxes or all shapes, for example), you can style them at the same time. To select multiple objects, touch and hold one object and then tap the other objects.

To style an object:

1 Tap the object to select it.

2 Tap 🔨 in the toolbar, and then tap Style (Figure 6.17).

3 To use a preset style, tap a style in the Style menu.

  The preset styles match the template you're using. The available style options vary by object type (text box, shape, or image). To return to the Style menu from any of the Style Options menus, tap ‹.

4 Tap Style Options at the bottom of the Style menu.

5 To change the fill color (for text boxes and shapes), tap Fill and then tap a color. Flick left or right to see all the colors.

6 To change the border color, width, or line type of a text box, shape, or image, tap Border and do any of the following (Figure 6.18):

  ▸ To add a border or picture frame, turn on Border.

  ▸ To choose a border color (text boxes and shapes), tap Color and then tap a color. Flick left or right to see all the colors.

  ▸ To change the thickness of the border (text boxes and shapes), drag the Width slider.

  ▸ To change the thickness of the picture frame (images), drag the Scale slider.

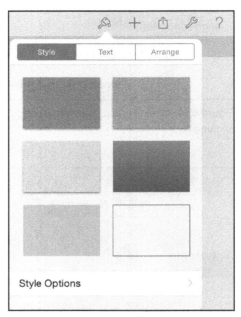

Figure 6.17 The Style menu.

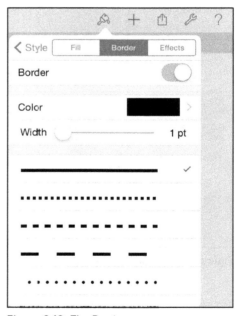

Figure 6.18 The Border menu.

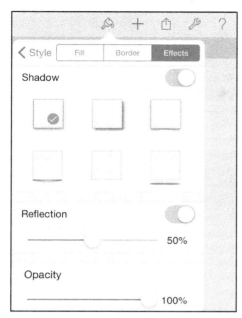

Figure 6.19 The Effects menu.

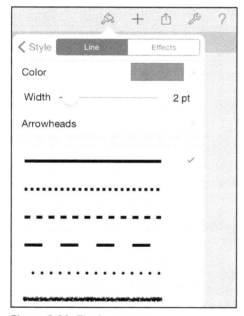

Figure 6.20 The Line menu.

▶ To choose a line type, tap one of the lines (solid, dotted, dashed, or charcoal). Flick up or down to see all the line types.

▶ To choose a picture frame style (images), tap a frame style. Flick up or down to see all the frame styles.

7 To change the shadow, reflection, or opacity of a text box, shape, or image, tap Effects and then do any of the following (Figure 6.19):

▶ To add a shadow, turn on Shadow and then tap a shadow style. (You should use the same shadow style for all objects, representing a single light source.)

▶ To make an image cast a reflection on the canvas, turn on Reflection and then drag the slider to adjust the reflection's translucence. Reflection works for objects and images.

▶ To make the object appear more or less solid, drag the Opacity slider. The lower the opacity, the more transparent the object.

8 To change the color, width, arrowheads, or line type of a line or arrow, tap Line and then do any of the following (Figure 6.20):

▶ To choose a line color, tap Color and then tap a color. Flick left or right to see all the colors.

▶ To change the thickness of the line, drag the Width slider.

▶ To change the arrowheads at either end of the line, tap Arrowheads and then select arrowhead styles.

▶ To choose a line type, tap one of the lines (solid, dotted, dashed, or charcoal). Flick up or down to see all the line types.

Arranging Objects

You can move, resize, rotate, flip, layer (stack), copy, and otherwise arrange objects on a sheet, though not all manipulations apply to all objects—you can't rotate or flip tables and charts, for example.

Selecting objects

When an object is selected, its selection handles ● are visible. If multiple selected objects are the same type (all text boxes or all shapes, for example), you can style them at the same time; see "Styling Objects" on page 108.

To select an object:

- Tap the object (Figure 6.21). (If the object is a table, tap ⊚ to select the entire table.)

To select multiple objects:

1 Touch and hold one object.

2 Tap the other objects (Figure 6.22). (If you tap an object accidentally, tap it again to deselect it.)

To select all objects on a sheet:

- Tap an empty area of the sheet (you may have to tap twice) and then tap Select All in the pop-up menu.

To deselect all objects:

- Tap an empty area of the sheet.

Figure 6.21 A selected object.

Figure 6.22 Selected objects.

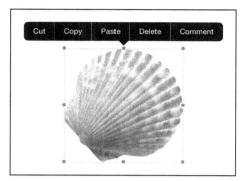

Figure 6.23 The Cut, Copy, and Delete commands.

Cutting, copying, and deleting objects

The Cut command removes the object so that it can be moved (pasted) elsewhere. Copy copies an object so that it can be duplicated (pasted) elsewhere, leaving the original object intact. Delete removes the object (without placing a copy on the clipboard).

If you select multiple objects, you can cut, copy, or delete them as a group.

To cut, copy, or delete an object:

1   Tap the object to select it, tap it again, and then tap Cut, Copy, or Delete in the pop-up menu (Figure 6.23). (If the object is a table, tap ⊙ to select the entire table.)

2   To paste a cut or copied object, go to the destination (which can be on the same sheet, on a different sheet, or on a sheet in a different spreadsheet), tap an empty area on the sheet, and then tap Paste in the pop-up menu.

Grouping objects

Grouping objects lets you move, resize, or rotate them as a single unit. A set of grouped objects can be grouped again with another set of grouped objects. Resizing a group that contains a text box won't resize the box's text.

To group objects:

1   Select all the objects that you want to group together (Figure 6.24).

2   Tap one of the selected objects, and then tap Group in the pop-up menu (Figure 6.25). (To ungroup a grouped object, tap it and then tap Ungroup in the pop-up menu.)

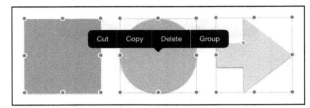

Figure 6.24 A selection of ungrouped objects.

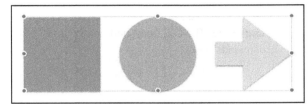

Figure 6.25 Grouped objects.

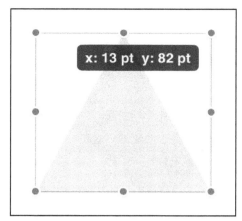

Figure 6.26 A pop-up label shows the object's position as you move it.

Moving objects

While you move or resize an object, **guides** flash on and off. These thin yellow lines help you align the center or edge of the object with other objects on the sheet. To turn guides on or off, tap ✐, and then tap Settings.

If you select multiple objects, you can drag them as a group.

To move an object:

- Select the object and drag it. (If the object is a table, drag ⊙ to move it.)

To nudge an object in fine increments:

- To nudge an object by one pixel, touch and hold the object with one finger, and then use another finger to flick across the sheet in the direction that you want the object to move.

  To nudge the object by 10, 20, or 30 pixels, flick with two, three, or four fingers.

  A pop-up label shows the object's x and y coordinates as you flick (Figure 6.26).

Resizing and reshaping objects

As you resize an object, center and edge guides appear and a pop-up label shows the dimensions of the resized object. You can resize an object from its edges or its center. Some shapes have extra, green selection handles ● that reshape and resize only certain parts of the shape.

To resize an object from an edge:

- Select the object and drag its selection handles ● (Figure 6.27).

To resize an object from its center:

1 Touch and hold a selection handle ● and, with a second finger, touch and hold an empty area on the sheet.

2 Drag the selection handle when the Center Resize label appears (Figure 6.28).

To make two objects the same size:

1 Select the object that you want to resize, and then drag a selection handle ●.

2 As you drag, touch and hold another object of the desired size.

3 When the Match Size label appears, lift your finger from the resized object (the first object) and then the other object, or lift both fingers at the same time (Figure 6.29).

To reshape an object:

- Select the object and drag its green selection handles ●, if present (Figure 6.30).

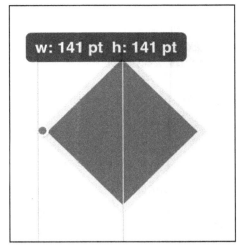

Figure 6.27 Resizing an object from its edge.

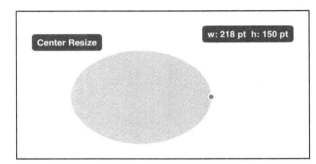

Figure 6.28 Resizing an object from its center.

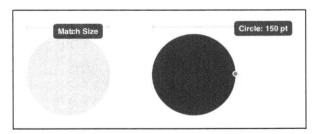

Figure 6.29 Making two objects the same size.

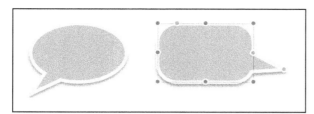
Figure 6.30 Original and reshaped objects.

Figure 6.31 Rotating an object.

Figure 6.32 Flipped images.

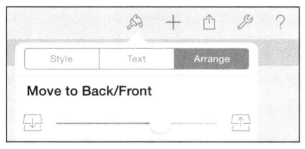
Figure 6.33 The Move to Back/Front slider.

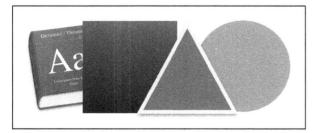
Figure 6.34 Layered objects.

Reorienting objects

You can rotate images, text boxes, and shapes. You can also flip images and change how overlapping objects are stacked bottom-to-top.

To rotate an object:

■ Place two fingers on an object and then rotate them clockwise or counter-clockwise. (If an image has transparency, don't hold its transparent areas.) After you've started the rotation, you can lift one finger and continue rotating by dragging a single finger.

You can rotate to any angle. During rotation, the object will snap into position at 45-degree increments, and the edge guide will brighten. A pop-up label shows the angle of rotation (Figure 6.31).

To flip an image:

■ Select the image, tap 🔨, tap Arrange, and then tap Flip Vertically or Flip Horizontally (Figure 6.32).

To layer an object:

■ Select the object (if the object is a table, tap ⊙ to select the entire table), tap 🔨, tap Arrange, and then drag the Move to Back/Front slider (Figure 6.33).

Dragging the slider left moves the object toward the bottom of the stack; dragging right moves it toward the top (Figure 6.34).

Locking objects

You can lock an object in place on the sheet, so that you can't change, move, or delete it accidently.

To lock an object:

- Select the object, tap ⚒, tap Arrange, and then tap Lock.

  The selection handles of a locked object change to ✖.

To unlock an object:

- Select the locked object, tap ⚒, and then tap Unlock.

CHAPTER 7

Sharing and Converting Spreadsheets

File sharing on an iPad isn't as simple as it is on Macs and PCs because the iPad has no centralized file storage area. You can't use drag-and-drop to transfer files between your iPad and computer, or open documents already on your iPad in any app you choose. Instead, each iPad app keeps its data in a sandbox: a private storage area that other apps can't see or change. You can use Apple's free iCloud service, however, to store, share, sync, or collaborate on spreadsheets online.

Tip: Numbers for iOS, Numbers for Mac (OS X), and Numbers for iCloud (*icloud.com*) all share the same unified file format.

Exporting and Importing Spreadsheets via iTunes

Using iTunes on your computer, you can:

- Export Numbers spreadsheets created on your iPad to make them available in iTunes (to, say, copy to your computer's hard drive and print or back up).

- Add spreadsheets from your computer to a special place in iTunes to import them to Numbers on your iPad over a USB connection.

Using iTunes to transfer document files isn't like syncing photos, videos, music, and apps between your computer and your iPad. iTunes doesn't sync documents; it copies them. Every copy operation to or from your iPad is a manual, one-way process—copies exist independently of one another. For example, if you create a document on your iPad and then copy it to your computer, any changes that you make in either copy won't replace or update the other.

Tip: To export a copy of a spreadsheet to another (compatible) app, open the spreadsheet that you want to copy, tap in the toolbar, and then tap Open in Another App.

To export a spreadsheet from your iPad to your computer:

1 On your iPad, open Numbers.

2 In the spreadsheet manager, open the spreadsheet that you want to export.

3 Tap in the toolbar, and then tap Send a Copy (Figure 7.1).

Figure 7.1 The Share menu.

Figure 7.2 The Choose a Format window.

Figure 7.3 The iTunes sidebar, showing a connected iPad.

4 Tap the file format that you want to use (Figure 7.2).

Numbers. The Numbers (.numbers) format is compatible with Numbers for iCloud and Numbers for Mac.

PDF. PDF files can be viewed and annotated on any popular operating system.

Excel. The Microsoft Excel 2007 (.xlsx) format is compatible with all modern spreadsheet programs and office suites.

CSV. The comma-separated values (.csv) format stores tabular data in plain-text form (meaning all formatting is lost). Each table in the spreadsheet is exported to a separate CSV file, containing a header row of field names (if defined) followed by one data record for each nonempty table row. Each record consists of fields separated by commas, and all records have an identical sequence of fields. CSV is a universal format and CSV files can be opened in any spreadsheet, database, text editor, word processor, accounting program, and more.

5 Tap iTunes.

6 Connect your iPad to your computer via a USB cable and then open iTunes on your computer.

7 In the iTunes sidebar or toolbar, click the icon for your iPad.

8 In the iTunes sidebar, click Apps under Settings (Figure 7.3), and then scroll to the File Sharing section at the bottom of the window.

9 In the Apps list under File Sharing, click Numbers.

10 In the Numbers Documents list (Figure 7.4), select the spreadsheet(s) that you want to copy to your computer. You can Control-click (or Command-click on the Mac) to select or deselect individual items, or Shift-click to select a contiguous range of items.

11 Drag the spreadsheet(s) from the Numbers Documents list to your desktop or another folder on your computer.

or

Click Save To, navigate to the destination folder, and then click Choose (or Select Folder).

iTunes copies the spreadsheet(s) to your computer.

Figure 7.4 The Numbers Documents list in iTunes.

To import a spreadsheet from your computer to your iPad:

1 Connect your iPad to your computer via a USB cable and then open iTunes on your computer.

2 In the iTunes sidebar or toolbar, click the icon for your iPad.

3 In the iTunes sidebar, click Apps under Settings, and then scroll to the File Sharing section at the bottom of the window.

4 In the Apps list under File Sharing, click Numbers.

5 Click Add File, locate and select the spreadsheet(s) that you want to import, and then click Choose (or Open).

or

Drag the spreadsheet(s) that you want to copy to your iPad from your desktop or from a folder window to the Numbers Documents list.

Tips for Importing Spreadsheets

- Numbers for iOS can open files formatted as Numbers for iCloud and Numbers '08 for Mac or later (.numbers), Microsoft Excel 97 and later (.xls, .xlsx), comma-separated values (.csv, .txt), and tab-delimited text files (.txt).

- Remove any special characters (such as the forward slash, "/") from file names before you import.

- If you have trouble importing an Excel file into Numbers, open the file in Excel, disable any encryption or security options, and then try to import it again.

- To delete items from the Copy from iTunes list, flick across a spreadsheet name, and then tap Delete.

- iTunes backs up your iPad automatically each time that you sync. These backups include files within Numbers. If you restore from one of these backups, your Numbers for iOS files will be restored. If you don't sync (that is, if you manage your iPad's content manually), then keep backup copies of your spreadsheets in a dedicated folder outside of iTunes.

- Importing an Excel spreadsheet strips it of features that Numbers doesn't support.

- To manage spreadsheets on your iPad, see "Spreadsheets" on page 12.

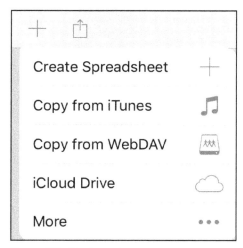

Figure 7.5 The Import menu.

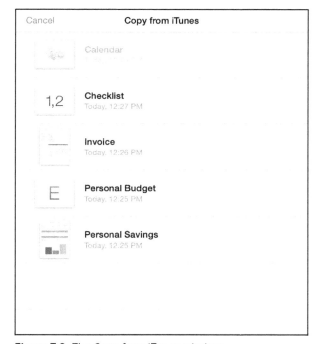

Figure 7.6 The Copy from iTunes window.

6   On your iPad, open Numbers.

7   In the spreadsheet manager, tap ➕ in the toolbar, and then tap Copy from iTunes (Figure 7.5).

8   In the Copy from iTunes window, tap the name of the spreadsheet that you want to import (Figure 7.6).

The spreadsheet opens and Numbers reports any problems that occurred during import. If Numbers can't find a closely matching font, it uses Helvetica.

Sending Copies of Spreadsheets

You can send copies of spreadsheet files from your iPad via email, Messages, or AirDrop. You can also open spreadsheets that you receive on your iPad. To send or receive spreadsheets, you must be connected to the internet and have your account set up on your iPad. Mail, Messages, and AirDrop setup are covered in the *iPad User Guide* at *help.apple.com/ipad*.

The following instructions explain how to send and receive spreadsheets via email.

Tip: To restrict access to a spreadsheet, password-protect it (page 19).

To send a spreadsheet in an email message from your iPad:

1 On your iPad, open Numbers.

2 Tap in the toolbar, and then tap Send a Copy (Figure 7.7).

   If you're in the spreadsheet manager, tap the spreadsheet that you want to send.

3 Tap the file format that you want to send: Numbers, PDF, Excel, or CSV.

4 Tap an option: Message, Mail, or AirDrop (if your device supports it).

   Other options, such as WebDAV (page 124) and iCloud (page 126) are also available.

5 In the email window that opens (Figure 7.8), type the email addresses of anyone to whom you want to send the spreadsheet. Type or paste the email addresses of your recipients in the To field, or tap ⊕ to add people from your contacts list. Optionally, type a message title and body in the Subject and body fields.

6 Tap Send.

Figure 7.7 The Share menu.

Figure 7.8 A spreadsheet attached to an outgoing email.

Figure 7.9 A spreadsheet attached to an incoming email.

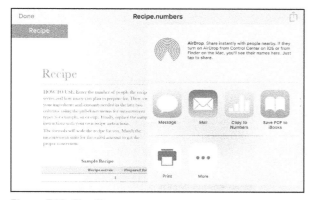

Figure 7.10 The Share menu.

To save a spreadsheet from an email message to your iPad:

1 On your iPad, open Mail.

2 Open the message containing the attached spreadsheet file (Figure 7.9). Attachments appear as icons in the body of the message.

3 If necessary, tap the file's icon to download it. The file size can give you an idea of how long the download will take.

4 When the download completes, tap the file's icon again.

    A preview of the spreadsheet opens in Mail.

5 In the toolbar at the top of the screen, tap ⬆ (Figure 7.10). (If the toolbar disappears, tap anywhere on the screen to bring it back.)

6 Print the spreadsheet (page 32) or open it in the desired app (which can be any app that can read or share Numbers files, not necessarily Numbers itself). Any of these actions saves the spreadsheet in the specified app.

Transferring Spreadsheets via Remote Server

You can copy your Numbers spreadsheets directly to or from a WebDAV server, if you have access to one. **WebDAV** (Web-based Distributed Authoring and Versioning) lets you easily upload and download large files, multiple files, or folders of files to specific sites.

You can transfer your spreadsheets in Numbers (.numbers), PDF (.pdf), Microsoft Excel (.xlsx), or CSV (.csv) file formats. You must first set up a server so that Numbers can access it. After signing in, you can copy files to or from the server until you tap Sign Out.

To set up your WebDAV server in Numbers:

1 In the spreadsheet manager, tap ➕ in the toolbar, tap Copy from WebDAV (Figure 7.11), and then type the server address (web address or URL), your user name, and password.

2 Tap Sign In in the top-right corner of the window.

Tip: You remain signed in to the server you set up until you tap Sign Out. To sign in to a different WebDAV server, sign out of the current server and then set up another one.

To copy a spreadsheet to a WebDAV server:

1 On your iPad, open Numbers.

2 Tap 🔼 in the toolbar, and then tap Send a Copy (Figure 7.12).

   If you're in the spreadsheet manager, tap the spreadsheet that you want to export.

3 Tap the file format that you want to export: Numbers, PDF, Excel, or CSV.

4 Tap WebDAV.

5 In the list of folders, tap the one in which you want to save the spreadsheet.

6 Tap Copy in the top-right corner of the window.

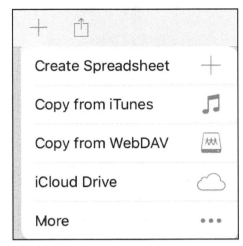

Figure 7.11 The Import menu.

Figure 7.12 The Share menu.

To copy a spreadsheet from a WebDAV server:

1 In the spreadsheet manager, tap ✛ in the tool-bar, and then tap Copy from WebDAV.

2 If necessary, navigate to the spreadsheet you want to copy by tapping the folder in which it's located.

3 Tap the spreadsheet that you want to copy.

 The spreadsheet downloads and appears in the spreadsheet manager.

To delete a file from a WebDAV server:

1 Access a list of files on a WebDAV server, ac-cording to the instructions above.

2 Flick across the file name and then tap Delete.

Tip: You can't undo this action or use this method to delete folders.

Storing Spreadsheets in iCloud

iCloud is an online storage and computing service that uploads (copies) your content to Apple's remote data center and pushes it wirelessly to your devices. iCloud stores your spreadsheets and keeps them up to date across your iOS devices, your Mac, and the web, so that you always have the most current versions at hand, no matter which device you used to make your latest edits. After you set up iCloud on your iOS device and Mac, every time that you edit a spreadsheet in Numbers on one device, your changes are automatically sent to your other devices where you've installed Numbers and turned on iCloud.

If you have newer devices, you can use **iCloud Drive** to share and sync spreadsheets. iCloud Drive requires iOS 8 or later on an iPhone, iPad, or iPod touch, OS X 10.10 Yosemite or later on a Mac, and Windows 7 or later on a PC. iCloud Drive completely replaces **Documents & Data** storage found in earlier operating systems. Upgrading to iCloud Drive is an optional, irreversible, one-time process. If you're using a new device with iOS 9 or later or OS X 10.11 El Capitan or later, iCloud Drive is turned on automatically. For details, read the Apple support articles "Use iWork with iCloud Drive" at *support.apple.com/ht201385* and "iCloud Drive FAQ" at *support.apple.com/ht201104*.

You can also create and edit Numbers spreadsheets in a web browser by using the **Numbers for iCloud** web app at *icloud.com*. Spreadsheets created using Numbers for iCloud are automatically available across your Macs and iOS devices that are set up to use iCloud—and vice versa: if you create a spreadsheet by using Numbers on an iOS device or Mac, it appears automatically on the web in Numbers for iCloud.

Tip: Numbers for iCloud is supported in these browsers: Safari 6.0.3 or later (Mac), Internet Explorer 10.0.9 or later (Windows), and Google Chrome 27.0.1 or later (Windows or Mac).

A few iCloud tips:

- If you edit and close a spreadsheet while you're not connected to the internet (offline), a ⬆ in the spreadsheet's thumbnail image indicates that the edited spreadsheet will be uploaded as soon as you connect to the internet (Figure 7.13).

- An uploaded spreadsheet is accompanied by a history of the edits that you made ("deltas", in geekspeak), so when you open the spreadsheet on another device, you can undo individual edits, just as if you had made the edits on that device.

- If you rename, delete, or password-protect a spreadsheet on one device, the change syncs across all your devices.

- If you organize your spreadsheets into folders on one device, all your devices are updated to reflect the same folder organization.

- You can download spreadsheets from the iCloud Numbers spreadsheet manager (*icloud.com*) to your Mac or Windows PC in Numbers, PDF, or Excel format.

- You can drag and drop Numbers, Excel, or CSV files from your Mac or Windows PC to the iCloud Numbers spreadsheet manager (*icloud.com*) to have them appear on your iOS devices automatically.

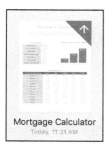

Mortgage Calculator
Today, 11:21 AM

Figure 7.13 An arrow indicates an unsynced spreadsheet.

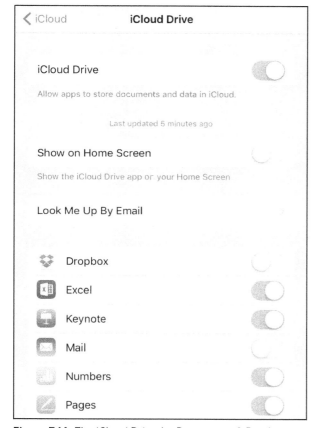

Figure 7.14 The iCloud Drive (or Documents & Data) screen in Settings.

Figure 7.15 In Settings, turn on iCloud for Numbers.

To set up iCloud in Numbers on your iOS device:

1 On the Home screen, tap Settings.

2 On the left side of the Settings screen, tap iCloud.

3 If necessary, sign in using your Apple ID, or request a new Apple ID and then sign in.

4 On the right side of the Settings screen, in the list of iCloud services, tap iCloud Drive (or Documents & Data).

5 Turn on iCloud Drive (or Documents & Data) and Numbers (Figure 7.14).

6 On the left side of the Settings screen, scroll down and then tap Numbers.

7 On the right side of the Settings screen, turn on Use iCloud (Figure 7.15).

Tip: When iCloud is turned off in Numbers on your device, edits that you make or new spreadsheets that you create in Numbers aren't automatically pushed to iCloud storage, and new or changed spreadsheets uploaded from other devices or from your computer aren't automatically available in Numbers on this device.

Sharing spreadsheets via iCloud

If you save a spreadsheet to iCloud (rather than locally on your device), you can send a link to it to others, who can open the spreadsheet in a supported browser to view or edit on OS X or Windows. Everyone with a link to the spreadsheet can see the changes (unless you password-protect it). iCloud syncs the spreadsheet across your iOS devices, your Mac, and the web, so everyone always has the latest version.

Tip: Collaborators don't need an iCloud account to view or edit the spreadsheet.

In the spreadsheet manager, a spreadsheet shared via iCloud is marked with 👤 (Figure 7.16). After iCloud sharing is turned on, you can resend the link as many times as you like.

To share a spreadsheet link:

1 Tap 📤 in the toolbar and then tap Share Link via iCloud (Figure 7.17).

   If you're in the spreadsheet manager, tap the spreadsheet that you want to share.

2 Tap a permissions option. "Allow editing" lets recipients change the spreadsheet on the web. "View only" lets recipients view (but not change) the spreadsheet on the web. All recipients can print and download the spreadsheet.

3 To require a password to open the spreadsheet, tap Add Password. If the spreadsheet already has a password, you can give the existing password to your recipients or tap Change Password.

4 Tap Share and then tap the method that you want to use to send the link (AirDrop, Message, Mail, Twitter, Facebook, and so on) (Figure 7.18).

   The full link appears in the body of the email, tweet, or post (don't change the link).

5 Enter the requested information and then send the link.

   Any further edits that you make to the spreadsheet are visible to all recipients of the link.

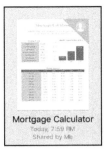

Figure 7.16 A spreadsheet shared via iCloud.

Figure 7.17 The Share menu.

Figure 7.18 The Share via iCloud window.

Tip: The Share menu also lets you copy the spreadsheet link to paste into a different app.

Figure 7.19 Tap View Share Settings.

Figure 7.20 The Share via iCloud window.

To view or edit sharing settings:

1 Open the spreadsheet, tap 👤 in the toolbar, and then tap View Share Settings (Figure 7.19).

2 Tap a sharing setting (Figure 7.20).

You can change permissions, add or change the password, remove the password, resend the link, copy the link (to paste elsewhere), or stop sharing.

---

iCloud on a Mac or Windows PC

If you're using iCloud on a Mac or Windows PC, you must set it up separately on your computer:

- On OS X, choose > System Preferences > iCloud.

- On Windows, download and install iCloud for Windows from *support.apple.com/ ht204283*.

Troubleshooting iCloud

If a spreadsheet was edited on two mobile devices before being updated on either device.

If you edit a spreadsheet on one mobile device and then edit that same spreadsheet on another device before the latest version has been pushed from the first device, then you will get a version conflict.

A Resolve Conflict window appears asking you to decide which versions of the spreadsheet you want to keep. Tap the circle next to each version of the spreadsheet that you want to keep, and then tap "Keep 1" or "Keep Both" in the top-right corner of the window. (If more than two versions of the spreadsheet are available, then you can select as many versions as you want; the Keep button reflects the number of spreadsheets selected.)

If you select more than one version of the spreadsheet, then all versions are saved to the current device. A number is appended to the spreadsheet's filename, so that no two files have the same name. For example, if you keep two versions of a spreadsheet named "Budget", then they appear as "Budget" and "Budget 1". All the saved versions of the conflicted spreadsheet are automatically pushed to your other mobile devices, keeping the files the same across devices.

If you can't open a spreadsheet displaying a downward-pointing arrow.

If you're not connected to the internet, then you might not be able to open an older spreadsheet that you haven't opened recently. This happens when the memory on your device becomes full so that it can't store all the spreadsheets that are available through iCloud. The older spreadsheets are temporarily suspended from the overloaded device to make space for those that have been viewed more recently.

To solve this problem, connect to the internet, and then try opening the spreadsheet again. The spreadsheet becomes a recently viewed spreadsheet, and another older spreadsheet is suspended from your device to make space for it. Alternatively, delete music, photos, videos, apps, or other items stored on your device to free up space for your spreadsheets.

If a newly created or edited spreadsheet isn't uploaded to iCloud.

Your iCloud storage space may be full. The new spreadsheet remains on your device, and is uploaded to iCloud when space becomes available. To create new iCloud storage space, delete one or more spreadsheets from your device, which also deletes them from iCloud and frees space for new spreadsheets. Alternatively, you can buy more iCloud storage space for an annual fee.

Index

www.ingramcontent.com/pod-product-compliance
Lightning Source LLC
Chambersburg PA
CBHW080425060326
40689CB00019B/4377